UNLOCKING
Wealth *from the*
COURTS OF HEAVEN

Destiny Image Books by Robert Henderson

Operating in the Courts of Heaven

Receiving Healing from the Courts of Heaven

Unlocking Destinies from the Courts of Heaven

Accessing the Courts of Heaven

Prayers and Declarations that Open the Courts of Heaven

The Books of Heaven

UNLOCKING
Wealth *from the*
COURTS OF HEAVEN

SECURING BIBLICAL PROSPERITY FOR KINGDOM
ADVANCEMENT AND GENERATIONAL BLESSING

ROBERT
HENDERSON

DESTINY IMAGE® PUBLISHERS, INC.

P.O. Box 310, Shippensburg, PA 17257-0310

"Promoting Inspired Lives."

This book and all other Destiny Image and Destiny Image Fiction books are available at Christian bookstores and distributors worldwide.

Cover design by Eileen Rockwell

For more information on foreign distributors, call 717-532-3040.

Reach us on the Internet: www.destinyimage.com.

ISBN 13 TP: 978-0-7684-4318-9

ISBN 13 eBook: 978-0-7684-5412-3

ISBN 13 HC: 978-0-7684-5414-7

ISBN 13 LP: 978-0-7684-5413-0

For Worldwide Distribution, Printed in the U.S.A.

2 3 4 5 6 7 8 / 24 23 22 21 20

CONTENTS

FOREWORD

In the early 1980s, the Lord invited my husband and I to leave our secular places of employment and follow Him into missionary work that included a life of trusting Him for supernatural provision with no visible means of financial support. He made it clear in that season that we were to inform no one of our needs but to go only to Him for help (to this very day we do not inform people of our personal needs).

When He issued the invitation, I was actually full of extreme faith and excitement. We were eager to step into this new season and had great expectation for the abundant life promised in scripture, believing it would manifest on a daily basis. We had heard many firsthand testimonies regarding sovereign, supernatural provision from friends and missionary acquaintances. We had also carefully and diligently studied the Bible from Genesis through to Revelation and embraced every beautiful promise of God's abundant supply that would meet our every need. Nowhere in the Word did we find any indication of God refusing to provide for those He loved and who walked according to His purposes. We clearly saw that it was God's will for His people to prosper with overflow in every area of our lives. We were completely confident that as we obeyed God, He would supernaturally supply. Joyful expectation filled our hearts and we stepped out to obey His invitation.

Very soon into this new season, we came to realize that the release of the miracle provision we were believing for failed to manifest without a strong "fight of faith." For five years, we fought that fight daily while being faithful and diligent to fulfill all the instruction in the Word regarding provision. We never missed a tithe, we gave offerings, we were faithful stewards, and walked in wisdom. We did not use credit cards or incur debt and we lived humbly. However, there were some very difficult challenges where some days we even lacked food for our household (although food always showed up before we bedded down each night). As challenging as the season was, we knew we had no other option but to obey God—we had no "Plan B." Every day we decreed the Word, and yet the word seemed to fall to the ground unfulfilled.

We remained in the faithful, grueling battle for five long years, and then one day, in a moment, everything broke for us. As a shift took place in the spirit, a realm of abundance was opened up that we are enjoying to this very day. Decades later we remain established in God's realms of riches and wealth. He truly came to give us all an abundant life.

After reading Robert Henderson's book, *Unlocking Wealth from the Courts of Heaven*, I am convinced that if we had understood the powerful insights contained in this book back in the beginning of our journey, our battle would not have been so long and grueling.

I often meet wonderful, precious believers who struggle terribly with lack and poverty. They are faithful to God to obey His Word yet fail to secure their breakthrough. We know for sure that this oppression and struggle is not God's will for them and therefore there must be an answer! I believe that important keys to help finally burst through walls of resistance are found in *Unlocking Wealth from the Courts of Heaven*. This book is not only built on solid scripture foundations but is loaded with the faith-building testimonies of many who have experienced breakthrough.

Are you struggling? Begin to rejoice. Things can shift for you quickly as you apply the teachings in this book.

Are you expecting greater release of God's riches and wealth in your life? You also will enjoy the insights that will open the doors for increase for you.

Thank you, Robert Henderson, for co-laboring with Christ to release this wonderful gift to His people.

—Patricia King

CHAPTER 1

WEALTH: GOD'S MANDATE

As I have progressed in my function in the Courts of Heaven, I have discovered that most all aspects of life can be addressed from this realm. I believe that the devil, our archenemy, uses legal issues in the spirit world to resist our obtaining all that Jesus died for us to have. This includes prosperity, wealth, and riches. First Peter 5:8 is clear that Satan uses legal arguments against us to devour and steal away what is rightfully ours on all levels.

> Be sober, be vigilant; because your adversary the devil walks about like a roaring lion, seeking whom he may devour.

The word *adversary* is the Greek word *antidikos*. It means "one who brings a lawsuit or is a legal opponent." Satan's efforts to devour us always have a legal right he claims to have discovered attached to them. He is *walking about* looking for any rights he can gain to seek to devour, destroy, or at least limit what we can have. *Walking about* implies his searching for anything legal that would grant him the right to consume and devour. Furthermore, the word *antidikos* comes from two words, *anti* and *dikos*. *Anti* means *instead of or against*. *Dikos* means *rights*. So the purpose behind Satan's legal attempts against us it to *deny us what is rightfully ours!* In other words, Satan uses legal issues against us to deny us what Jesus' death, burial, resurrection, and ascension gained for us. This is why in spite of Jesus' work on our behalf people still die prematurely, experience calamity, see families destroyed, and other traumatic things occur. This definitely is true when it comes to us prospering as God's people. Prosperity, riches, and wealth are a part of our covenant rights and expectations. We are told that when Jesus died on the cross, He *became poor that we might be rich*. This is seen in Second Corinthians 8:9.

> For you know the grace of our Lord Jesus Christ, that though He was rich, yet for your sakes He became poor, that you through His poverty might become rich.

Jesus becoming poor does not speak of the life He lived while functioning and ministering in the earth. Jesus was not poor. He wore a robe that the soldiers gambled for because it was so expensive (see John 19:24). Jesus had a money bag with wealth in it. Why else would Judas have been stealing from it (see John 12:6)? Rich and influential people took care of Him and the disciples with great substance (see Luke 8:2-3). Jesus being poor instead speaks of His allowing Himself to be stripped and abused on the cross. When Jesus hung on the cross, He defeated among other things the spirit of poverty, lack, and need. He took it upon Himself so we could be *rich*. Jesus made a trade on our behalf. He took poverty on Himself so we could be freed to be rich.

The word *rich* is the Greek word *plouteo*. It means "to be or become wealthy, to increase in goods, to wax rich." Everything Jesus did on the cross was foreshadowed by the Israelites coming out of Egypt. When they came forth from Egypt as the judgment of God came on that land but *passed over* them, three significant things happened. Psalm 105:36-38 tells us these three prominent things as God brought His people out of the bondage of Egypt.

> *He also destroyed all the firstborn in their land,*
> *The first of all their strength.*
> *He also brought them out with silver and gold,*
> *And there was none feeble among His tribes.*
> *Egypt was glad when they departed,*
> *For the fear of them had fallen upon them.*

First, judgment was rendered that set them free from the bondage of slavery. As the final plague entered Egypt and killed the firstborn, all who had the blood of the Passover lamb on their homes escaped this terror. God through His judgment on Egypt broke the power of their strength to hold His people captive. As God's judgment came on this godless nation, His people in the midst of them were set free. The blood of the Passover lamb prohibited the judgment from touching any of them who had heard and obeyed the mandate to place the blood on their homes. The blood is what makes us His covenant people. When the blood was seen, that which would destroy thousands of Egyptians would not touch God's covenant people marked by the blood. This speaks of our spiritual salvation that will not allow judgment to touch us. The blood of Jesus, our Passover Lamb, will not allow it. First Thessalonians 5:9 gives us the wonderful promise that the wrath to come will not come close to us.

> For God did not appoint us to wrath, but to obtain salvation through our Lord Jesus Christ.

God's wrath against sinners will not be able to affect us. However, we have and will obtain salvation through our Lord Jesus Christ and all that He has done for us. The second thing that was foreshadowed in Egypt was healing for our bodies. The scripture says there was *none feeble among His tribes.* This means that everyone was healed of their weakness, infirmity, and sickness. Millions of Jews were instantly healed because of the covenant they entered through the body and blood of the Passover lamb. In addition to the blood being placed on the doorpost of each home that secured their salvation from the wrath of judgment, they also ate the carcass of the Passover lamb. Exodus 12:7-8 declares this reality.

> *And they shall take some of the blood and put it on the two doorposts and on the lintel of the houses where they eat it. Then they shall eat the flesh on that night; roasted in fire, with unleavened bread and with bitter herbs they shall eat it.*

As the blood was placed on the doorpost of their house, salvation from the judgment was secured. When they ate the flesh of the roasted lamb, however, healing was obtained. This is why there was *none feeble* among them. Isaiah 53:4 clearly tells us that when Jesus died on the cross in His body, He carried and bore away our sickness and diseases.

> *Surely He has borne our griefs*
> *And carried our sorrows;*
> *Yet we esteemed Him stricken,*
> *Smitten by God, and afflicted.*

The word *grief* is the Hebrew word *choliy* and it means "malady, calamity, disease, and sickness." The word *sorrows* is the Hebrew word *makob* and it means "anguish, affliction, grief, and pain." When this scripture was translated into the New Testament in Matthew 8:16-17, it shows that Jesus would bring healing to the sick and diseased.

> *When evening had come, they brought to Him many who were demon-possessed. And He cast out the spirits with a word, and healed all who were sick, that it might be fulfilled which was spoken by Isaiah the prophet, saying:*
>
> *"He Himself took our infirmities*
> *And bore our sicknesses."*

Even prior to the cross, Jesus was drawing from what He would do on the cross. The Father allowed this, because He was *slain before the foundations of the earth* (see Revelation 13:8). In other words, in the mind and heart of God He had already offered His Son for the redemption of His creation. So when, prior to the cross, Jesus healed people on the basis of His sacrifice, He was drawing from what He had already done in the mind of the Father. The main thought here, however, is that it was the offering of His body on the cross that secured healing. This is why when even in a foreshadow the children of Israel ate the flesh of the Passover lamb, they were healed. There was none who were even feeble among them. This is one of the main benefits of His salvation for us even seen in the exodus from Egypt.

The third significant thing that occurred as the people of God left Egypt was they left rich! The scripture we saw says *"He also brought them out with silver and gold."* Moses commanded the people of God to ask of the Egyptians all their stuff. Exodus 12:35-36 says the Israelites asked the Egyptians for their wealth. They actually gave it to them. They were so ready for them to leave they gave them whatever they wanted.

> *Now the children of Israel had done according to the word of Moses, and they had asked from the Egyptians articles of silver, articles of gold, and clothing. And the Lord had given the people favor in the sight of the Egyptians, so that they granted them what they requested. Thus they plundered the Egyptians.*

They left with the silver and gold from Egypt. This was a great wealth transfer that happened that was a part of the salvation of the Jews from Egypt. It is a picture for us of what we can expect when we enter the covenant with our God through the body and blood of the Passover Lamb. Not only do we obtain spiritual salvation and bodily healing, we also can move from poverty to riches and prosperity. This is what happened to the Israelites. In a night they went from poverty-stricken slaves to wealthy Jews. This occurred because of the favor God granted them in the sight of the Egyptians as a result of His salvation afforded them. We too can expect this kind of favor as a part of our salvation. *He became poor for us that we might become rich.* If this is true, which it is because it is based on the covenant-keeping nature of God and His Word, then why are so many not experiencing this? It is because the devil has a legal case set against you to *deny you what is rightfully yours.* If we are to prosper as we are told we are, then we must be able to undo any legal right the devil is yet claiming to have. This requires us stepping into the Courts of Heaven and learning to function in this regard. To do this we first need at least a basic understanding of the Courts of Heaven.

The idea of there being a Court in Heaven is seen throughout scripture. Anytime we read of the Throne of God, we are actually reading about not just a place of worship but a place of judicial activity. We see the Court of Heaven revealed the most clearly in Daniel 7:9-10.

> *I watched till thrones were put in place,*
>
> *And the Ancient of Days was seated;*
>
> *His garment was white as snow,*
>
> *And the hair of His head was like pure wool.*
>
> *His throne was a fiery flame,*

Its wheels a burning fire;

A fiery stream issued

And came forth from before Him.

A thousand thousands ministered to Him;

Ten thousand times ten thousand stood before Him.

The court was seated,

And the books were opened.

Daniel is watching as a *seer* in the spirit world. He *sees* the realm of Heaven and a *court* that is there. The first thing we must know about the Court of Heaven is it isn't a method of praying but a spiritual dimension. Don't let this scare you or seem to refuse you a right to function there. We are called by God to stand by faith in these spiritual places. This is a part of our heritage as New Testament believers. Just like Daniel saw and functioned in this Court, so we are allowed this place as well. This is what Hebrews 12:22-24 is teaching us. We are being shown that we as New Testament people have been repositioned in a spiritual dimension we must by faith operate in. We must take God at His word and simply begin to move in these realms.

> *But you have come to Mount Zion and to the city of the living God, the heavenly Jerusalem, to an innumerable company of angels, to the general assembly*

and church of the firstborn who are registered in
heaven, to God the Judge of all, to the spirits of just
men made perfect, to Jesus the Mediator of the new
covenant, and to the blood of sprinkling that speaks
better things than that of Abel.

The writer is telling us *where we have come to.* This means he is exposing the place we have been given in the realm of the spirit. When you look at what is mentioned here you will see that there is a legal connotation to these things. First of all, we have come to Mount Zion. Anytime we read about a *mountain* in the Bible, we are reading about something that is governmental and judicial. The prophet Isaiah promised in Isaiah 56:7 to bring us to God's *holy mountain* and make us joyful in His house of prayer.

Even them I will bring to My holy mountain,

And make them joyful in My house of prayer.

Their burnt offerings and their sacrifices

Will be accepted on My altar;

For My house shall be called a house of prayer for
all nations.

The *holy mountain* is not describing a geographical place but rather a spiritual dimension. When you connect Hebrews 12:22-24 with Isaiah 56:7, we see that a people of prayer are allowed by God to stand in a *mountain* in the spirit world and function there. All the other activities mentioned in Hebrews 12:22-24 are the heavenly functions that are occurring in this spiritual place called a *mountain*. Blood speaking/testifying, Jesus mediating the New Covenant, spirits of just men, God the Judge, the legal people of God called an ecclesia/church, and other things are all actions and activities in this spiritual place called a *mountain*. What we are seeing here is the place we have been granted as New Testament believers to stand in. We are positioned in a heavenly realm called a mountain, *where* the Court of Heaven functions. Notice too that *we have come* to this place. I tell people quite often that the people of God have a problem. We keep trying to *get* to a place we have already *come to*. This is where faith comes in. We take God at His word and believe we are positioned in a heavenly place called a *mountain* where the Courts of Heaven operate. When we by faith accept and acknowledge the truth of this, we are now ready to function there, agree with the activity present in this unseen realm, and get our breakthrough.

Many things can be done in and from the Courts of Heaven. In fact, I have discovered that almost anything we desire from the Lord and is in agreement with His will and purposes can be secured from this realm. This includes the unlocking of wealth, riches, and prosperity.

We simply need to learn how to present our case in these Courts to see the release of what has been held up. So many people struggle financially. They have sought to discover principles that would allow them and their families to come into the abundance God's Word promises. Yet they remain limited and hindered in this endeavor. It is my sincere belief and understanding that what hasn't happened through just hard work and even faithfulness to other biblical principles can be unlocked and released from the Courts of Heaven. Let us go on this journey together and perhaps see any history of lack, need, insufficiency, and even poverty end. Let's step into a future filled with a sufficiency in all things and an abundance for every good work. Second Corinthians 9:8 reflects this idea.

And God is able to make all grace abound toward you, that you, always having all sufficiency in all things, may have an abundance for every good work.

What would life be like with all needs met, longings fulfilled, and an ability to bless *every good work?* For many it would be a dream come true. I'm here to tell you God is faithful. He hasn't destined you to a life of survival, just enough, or even not enough. He has destined you to live in the fullness of who He is and His resources. God is the God of the open hand according to Psalm 145:15-16.

The eyes of all look expectantly to You,

And You give them their food in due season.

You open Your hand

And satisfy the desire of every living thing.

The Lord is not stingy, restrictive, or withholding. He delights to satisfy His creation with good things and abundance. Through the Courts of Heaven, we can see any legal right the devil is claiming revoked. We can present our case in agreement with God's Word and promises. We will move from something being just a dream to the reality of it manifesting. We can and will see wealth unlocked from the Courts of Heaven!

Lord, as I come before You, I ask for the wisdom and understanding to stand in Your Courts, even the Courts of Heaven. I ask, Lord, that You would grant me insight in how to function in this dimension and realm. I thank You, Lord, that from the place of the Spirit I will be able to see unlocked the wealth and prosperity that You would apportion to me and my family. Thank You, Lord, that You are the God of abundance and You desire to bless us in an abounding way. My hope, Lord, is in You as I stand and petition Your Courts for the prosperity You have for me. In Jesus' Name, amen.

CHAPTER 2

APPROACHING THE JUDICIAL
SYSTEM OF HEAVEN

A s we endeavor to *unlock wealth from the Courts of Heaven*, we must have an awareness of *how* to approach this place in the spirit. Jesus taught much on prayer. However, in Luke 18:1-8 when speaking on prayer, He placed it in a judicial setting.

> *Then He spoke a parable to them, that men always ought to pray and not lose heart, saying: "There was in a certain city a judge who did not fear God nor regard man. Now there was a widow in that city; and she came to him, saying, 'Get justice for me from my adversary.' And he would not for a while; but afterward he said within himself, 'Though I do not fear God nor regard man, yet because this widow troubles me I will avenge her, lest by her continual coming she weary me.'"*

> *Then the Lord said, "Hear what the unjust judge said. And shall God not avenge His own elect who cry out day and night to Him, though He bears long with them? I tell you that He will avenge them speedily. Nevertheless, when the Son of Man comes, will He really find faith on the earth?"*

As I have shared many times, Jesus was *not* saying God is an unjust God we have to convince to move on our behalf. Jesus' point was that *if* this widow with no power, influence, wealth, or means to *buy* her favor from this unjust judge could get a verdict on her behalf, how much more can we go before the *righteous Judge* and see Him render a verdict on behalf of us, His elect? However, we must recognize that Jesus, by placing this account in a judicial system, was affirming to us that we must know how to tread His Courts. We must know how to operate within the protocol of this heavenly dimension. A very real part of prayer is knowing how to present a legal petition before the Court of Heaven.

In this story Jesus told, there are some very interesting things to consider. First of all, Jesus spoke this parable to encourage us to not stop praying. The worst thing you can do when it seems prayer isn't working is to stop. The solution to what would seem to be ineffective praying is not to stop but to adjust. Jesus actually placed prayer in three dimensions. Approaching God as Judge is the third dimension He taught. The other two dimensions are found in Luke 11:1-8 where Jesus taught approaching God as Father and Friend. In Luke 11:2 we see Jesus teaching us to approach God as Father.

> *So He said to them, "When you pray, say:*
> *Our Father in heaven,*
> *Hallowed be Your name.*
> *Your kingdom come.*
> *Your will be done*
> *On earth as it is in heaven."*

Approaching God as Father is basic to all praying. We will never go any deeper in prayer than our revelation of God as Father allows. Romans 8:15 tells us that it is the Spirit of adoption that creates a revelation and cry to God as Father.

> *For you did not receive the spirit of bondage again to*
> *fear, but you received the Spirit of adoption by whom*
> *we cry out, "Abba, Father."*

The Spirit of adoption is a reference to the Holy Spirit. The person of the Holy Spirit comes into our heart and from revelation creates the cry of Abba Father. We know

God is our Father and it empowers a life of prayer. The second dimension of prayer is approaching God as Friend. We see Jesus teaching this in Luke 11:5-8.

> *And He said to them, "Which of you shall have a friend, and go to him at midnight and say to him, 'Friend, lend me three loaves; for a friend of mine has come to me on his journey, and I have nothing to set before him'; and he will answer from within and say, 'Do not trouble me; the door is now shut, and my children are with me in bed; I cannot rise and give to you'? I say to you, though he will not rise and give to him because he is his friend, yet because of his persistence he will rise and give him as many as he needs."*

Jesus is showing us how to approach God as our Friend and secure for others breakthrough on their behalf. We know this because Jesus pictures a *friend* standing between two *friends*. One has a need while the other has resources. It is the *friend* in the middle who secures resources from one *friend* (God) for another *friend* (man with need). Approaching God as Friend is a place of intercession on behalf of another. This is the second realm of prayer Jesus taught.

The third realm of prayer of coming before the judicial system of Heaven and God as Judge of all is the key to unanswered prayer being answered. Jesus prefaced the story of the widow and the unjust judge with the statement about *not fainting or growing weary in prayer*. Jesus was not being a cheerleader. He was about to give the disciples instruction on what to do when answers did not come from the other two realms of praying. Jesus understood that the reason prayers are not answered is not because the Father isn't hearing or the Friend doesn't care. Unanswered prayer was because something legal in the spirit realm was resisting, just like the widow had an opponent. The widow's opponent was legal in nature. Remember the word *adversary* is the Greek word *antidikos*. It literally means one who brings a lawsuit. So the widow was petitioning the unjust judge to render a decision/verdict that would forbid her legal opponent from harassing her, stealing from her, or hurting her in some way. Her activity in this judicial setting was to be avenged of her legal opponent who was working against her. We, too, have a legal opponent working against us. In First Peter 5:8, Peter tells us that we must be on guard or our adversary/legal opponent will devise a legal case to devour us.

> *Be sober, be vigilant; because your adversary the devil walks about like a roaring lion, seeking whom he may devour.*

This word *adversary* in the Greek is the same word, *antidikos*. So the devil as our legal opponent is seeking to devise a means to devour us. This applies in every area of life. However, it definitely applies in the prosperity realm and God's desire and need for us to prosper. Satan does not want us prospering as God's people. He desires to keep us in bondage and survival mode. If he can do this, he will stifle our ability to expand the kingdom of God. He knows that if we only have time to think about and be worried concerning our own status, we will be distracted from being a part of the *increase of His government and peace in the earth*. This is what Isaiah 9:7 prophetically declares would be the agenda of Jesus and those of us who belong to Him.

> *Of the increase of His government and peace*
> *There will be no end,*
> *Upon the throne of David and over His kingdom,*
> *To order it and establish it with judgment and justice*
> *From that time forward, even forever.*
> *The zeal of the Lord of hosts will perform this.*

Since the days that Jesus came into the earth *announcing* the kingdom/government of God, God's rule in the earth has been increasing. Life on the planet is better today than it has ever been. In the midst of the challenges that we face, the government and rule of God continues to enlarge and impact nations. When Jesus entered the earth in the first century His declaration was *"the kingdom of God has come.* Matthew 4:23 tells us the kingdom and rule of God in the earth was Jesus' declaration, message, and announcement.

> *And Jesus went about all Galilee, teaching in their synagogues, preaching the gospel of the kingdom, and healing all kinds of sickness and all kinds of disease among the people.*

As Jesus made this proclamation, people were healed and lives restored. Healing was a physical depiction of the rule of God coming into people's lives. It's not the *only* depiction, but it was the *first* one that Jesus manifested to confirm to people the rule and government of God was in their midst. Prosperity, riches, and the accumulation of wealth is another manifestation that the government of God has come. Deuteronomy 8:18 clearly tells us that God *needs* a wealthy people to accomplish His purpose in the earth. That purpose is the *increase of His government and rule.*

> *And you shall remember the Lord your God, for it is He who gives you power to get wealth, that He may establish His covenant which He swore to your fathers, as it is this day.*

We are told from this scripture that the power to get wealth is for the establishment of God's covenant. This means what God has promised to do is the redemption of the earth and its inhabitants. This is the increase of the government of God. It cannot happen except through a wealthy people. So God is looking for those He can bless with wealth. The devil knows this. Therefore, he works to deny us the wealth God desires us to steward. Satan knows if he can do this, he can thwart the desire of God to see His kingdom enlarged. The plan of Satan to stop God's people from obtaining and stewarding wealth involves his discovering a legal right against us. This is the way he devours. This is realized as we understand more fully the term used to describe Satan and his function. Remember, he is the *adversary*, the *antidikos*. He is our legal opponent and one who brings a lawsuit. Remember the *antidikos* is seeking to deny us what is rightfully ours. As we previously saw when Jesus died on the cross, He removed the curse of poverty, lack, and need from us. However, the devil, our adversary/legal opponent, is yet seeking to build a case against us to deny us what is rightfully ours. We are called and designed by God to prosper, increase wealth, and even be rich. Yet so many cannot seem to come into this reality. The problem is not with God. The problem is the devil has searched out a case against us that is denying us what is rightfully ours. As we go before the Courts of Heaven, we can see this case demolished and our God-ordained right to prosper occur!

Another thing we can learn from the Luke 18:1-8 verses about operating in prayer in the Courts of Heaven—the Lord as Judge will require the devil to repay what he has stolen. As we look at these scriptures, notice that the widow's petition was for the adversary to be made to pay back. Luke 18:3 shows us this truth.

> *Now there was a widow in that city; and she came to him, saying, "Get justice for me from my adversary."*

Notice her request was *justice **from** her adversary*. She didn't just want things made right; she wanted her adversary to be made to pay up and experience the justice of the judicial system against him. In the Court of Heaven, we can actually take Satan and his forces to court and require them to give back what they have stolen and more. We see this in scripture. There are three references that come to mind. The first is in Proverbs 6:30-31.

> *People do not despise a thief*
> *If he steals to satisfy himself when he is starving.*
> *Yet when he is found, he must restore sevenfold;*
> *He may have to give up all the substance of his house.*

We know the devil is the *thief.* John 10:10 tells us that the thief, which is Satan, comes to steal, kill, and destroy.

The thief does not come except to steal, and to kill, and to destroy. I have come that they may have life, and that they may have it more abundantly.

Satan devises legal cases against us that allow him to steal everything that is precious from us. However, Jesus has come that we might have it all back plus more. When the thief is found out and discovered, he must repay sevenfold. This is the basis of God's word. We have a right to go before the Courts of Heaven and ask of our Judge for our adversary to give back everything he has taken from us. Not just what we lost but sevenfold what we lost. This is what the widow was doing. She didn't want to just get back whatever had been taken from her; she wanted it back and the adversary to suffer and experience lack!

The phrase *when he is found* is an important part of the process. This doesn't mean that we just realize we have lost something. It means we have discovered what allowed it to happen in the first place. In other words, what gave the devil the legal right to steal from us? Was it sin in my life? Perhaps transgression has been operating. Could this be it? Maybe it is iniquity and issues in my ancestral past. It could be that a covenant has been made with demon powers. Or even yet, could it be vows that were made or word curses operating? We will examine these things in later chapters, but just realize this is a part of the thief *being found.* When he *is found*, he will be required to give up all the resources of his house to pay back the judgment against him. This is what we can require in the Courts of Heaven. We don't just get back what was lost. We can get back up to sevenfold what was lost. This can be the justice of God in a matter.

We also see the adversary being made to restore in Job's life. Job had lost everything because Satan had brought an accusation and a case against him. He had accused Job of not serving God with a pure heart. Job 1:6-11 shows us this activity of Satan before the Court of Heaven and the accusation he brought against Job.

> *Now there was a day when the sons of God came to present themselves before the Lord, and Satan also came among them. And the Lord said to Satan, "From where do you come?"*
>
> *So Satan answered the Lord and said, "From going to and fro on the earth, and from walking back and forth on it."*
>
> *Then the Lord said to Satan, "Have you considered My servant Job, that there is none like him on the earth, a blameless and upright man, one who fears God and shuns evil?"*

So Satan answered the Lord and said, "Does Job fear God for nothing? Have You not made a hedge around him, around his household, and around all that he has on every side? You have blessed the work of his hands, and his possessions have increased in the land. But now, stretch out Your hand and touch all that he has, and he will surely curse You to Your face!"

Satan is moving around, going back and forth and to and fro. He is searching out and gathering evidence to gain a legal right to devour from. He brings an accusation against Job. His accusation is that Job only serves God because of the Lord's blessing on his life. The blessing is there because of a hedge or restraint that God has in place that will not let Satan touch him. The word *hedge* is the Hebrew word *suwk.* It means "a protection or restraint." It could clearly mean that God has a restraining order in place that will not allow the devil to come near him. This hedge that is in place has allowed Job to prosper beyond anyone else near him. We will deal more extensively with how to get this restraining order in place in a later chapter. This being in place will allow an atmosphere to be functioned in that will produce great wealth. He is a very blessed man with family, but also with provisions and prosperity. However, Satan brings a case against Job to cause the restraining and protective order to be lifted that

Satan might do Job damage and harm. We know that Job did lose almost everything. With regard to wealth we see that Job in *one day* lost much. Job 1:13-19 tells us all that he lost in what would seem a moment of time.

> *Now there was a day when his sons and daughters were eating and drinking wine in their oldest brother's house; and a messenger came to Job and said, "The oxen were plowing and the donkeys feeding beside them, when the Sabeans raided them and took them away—indeed they have killed the servants with the edge of the sword; and I alone have escaped to tell you!"*
>
> *While he was still speaking, another also came and said, "The fire of God fell from heaven and burned up the sheep and the servants, and consumed them; and I alone have escaped to tell you!"*
>
> *While he was still speaking, another also came and said, "The Chaldeans formed three bands, raided the camels and took them away, yes, and killed the servants with the edge of the sword; and I alone have escaped to tell you!"*
>
> *While he was still speaking, another also came and said, "Your sons and daughters were eating and drinking wine in their oldest brother's house, and suddenly a great wind came from across the wilderness*

and struck the four corners of the house, and it fell on the young people, and they are dead; and I alone have escaped to tell you!"

Through people stealing, storms arising, and enemies attacking, Job lost his wealth and his children in one day, if not one afternoon. Everything he had spent his entire life accumulating was gone in an instant. This all occurred because Satan brought a case against Job. Job actually realized he was in a court case before the Lord. He had some kind of awareness that an accusation had come against him that had allowed this. He also knew that only the court ruling in his favor could turn this situation around. Job 9:19 speaks of a time to plead for righteous judgment on his behalf.

If it is a matter of strength, indeed He is strong;

And if of justice, who will appoint my day in court?

Job wanted to know how he could get an appointed day in God's court to plead his case. In Job 9:15, Job speaks of asking mercy of his judge.

For though I were righteous, I could not answer Him;

I would beg mercy of my Judge.

Job understood that mercy from the Court of Heaven was a necessary thing. That he could not stand in his own righteousness before his Judge. We then see in Job 23:1-7, Job desiring a time when he might appear before the Lord and His seat.

> *Then Job answered and said:*
> *"Even today my complaint is bitter;*
> *My hand is listless because of my groaning.*
> *Oh, that I knew where I might find Him,*
> *That I might come to His seat!*
> *I would present my case before Him,*
> *And fill my mouth with arguments.*
> *I would know the words which He would answer me,*
> *And understand what He would say to me.*
> *Would He contend with me in His great power?*
> *No! But He would take note of me.*
> *There the upright could reason with Him,*
> *And I would be delivered forever from my Judge."*

Job understood deliverance from his circumstance and restoration could only come from presenting his case before His seat. He felt that if he could reason with the Lord as Judge, he would be delivered. Job had a clear concept that his deliverance and restoration to prosperity would have to come from the Court of Heaven. This is exactly what happened. We see in Job 42:10-17 the verdict of Heaven from the Courts Job desired to consult in, granting him complete restoration of property, prosperity, reputation, children, and long life. He was given back two times everything that was lost.

> And the Lord restored Job's losses when he prayed for his friends. Indeed the Lord gave Job twice as much as he had before. Then all his brothers, all his sisters, and all those who had been his acquaintances before, came to him and ate food with him in his house; and they consoled him and comforted him for all the adversity that the Lord had brought upon him. Each one gave him a piece of silver and each a ring of gold.

> Now the Lord blessed the latter days of Job more than his beginning; for he had fourteen thousand sheep, six thousand camels, one thousand yoke of oxen, and one thousand female donkeys. He also had seven sons and three daughters. And he called the name of the first Jemimah, the name of the second Keziah, and the name of the third Keren-Happuch. In all the land were found no women so beautiful as the daughters of Job; and their father gave them an inheritance among their brothers.

After this Job lived one hundred and forty years, and saw his children and grandchildren for four generations. So Job died, old and full of days.

Job's willingness to pray for his friends who had condemned him and spoke against him seems to be the final touches God from His Court needed to reward Job with twice what had been lost. When Job forgave and released any form of bitterness and anger toward his unwise friends, God reached a decision to bless Job. If we are to see restoration come, we must allow God to deal in our heart. We cannot hold grudges and wrath against others. This can prohibit God being able to release His twofold blessing back into our life. This was the activity of the Court of Heaven on behalf of Job that allowed his captivity to turn and his prosperity to return.

Jesus also spoke of the devil being made to repay what he has stolen. Mark 3:27 reveals Jesus speaking of binding the strong man and plundering his house.

No one can enter a strong man's house and plunder his goods, unless he first binds the strong man. And then he will plunder his house.

To plunder the strong man's house speaks of taking back what he has taken and stolen away. We must first *bind* this strong man, which is Satan in this situation. The

Greek word for *bind* is *deo*. Among other things it means "to prohibit and call to be unlawful." When we *bind* something, we are setting in place legal activity. Binding the strong man therefore is discovering and setting in place the legal rights granted to us from the Courts of Heaven and our activity there. Once this is done, we can plunder and take away all the resources the devil is holding in his *house*. All that he is illegally holding and controlling we now take back for the kingdom of God's sake. He is made to pay up.

This is what the widow was asking of the judge. *I want my adversary to be made to give back all that he has taken. I want my stuff back plus more.* When you understand this, you can come and stand in the Courts of Heaven and request justice on your behalf. When our request pleases the Lord, it will be granted to us.

Mary, my wife, and I have experienced this very thing. Several years ago, before I understood the Courts of Heaven, we went through devastating losses. We lost finances, reputation, family destinies, and some other things. It was not a good time. One of the things we lost was the dream home that Mary had designed and we had built. This was in Waco, Texas. We had built this home and in the process God had said to me, "This is My gift to you for your years of service to Me." I heard those words from God so very clearly. As I transitioned from pastoring

the church we had raised up to full-time itinerate ministry, we moved from Waco. The intention was to sell this
house, God's gift to us, and get things reset for the next
phase of our lives. After two years we decided it was time
to place this house on the market. In the meantime I had
been required to sign a document for some banking issues
concerning the ministry I was and still am the president
of. I signed the document at the request of the bank and
the person who needed to do business with this bank in
my absence. The problem was the papers were signed but
my authorization, without my awareness, had granted
this person the right to place my house as collateral on
the loan being renewed if he wanted to. This was done
without my knowledge whatsoever. This person obtained
for himself an additional $125,000 and used my house as
collateral for the loan. The end result was that when I sold
my house, the bank informed me the equity in the house
wasn't mine but would be placed on the debt of the ministry. In other words, we got *nothing* from the house that
God had given us as a gift and had been built with our
own money. Our house, God's gift, had been stolen away.

Needless to say, we struggled with bitterness, forgive-
ness, and anger. God helped us find His grace to forgive.
Yet we were still absent our house and the money that
would have come from it. During this season of my life,
prophets would come to me and declare that God was

going to restore everything double that had been lost. It brought some comfort, but we were still struggling under the sting of loss and the wrong things people believed about us. Fast-forward about 10 years and God begins to speak to me about moving back to Waco. There were dreams, words, impressions, and clear directions that this was what we were to do. However, as a result of all that had transpired in that place, I really didn't want to head-quarter there as a ministry or live there as a family. Yet God kept dealing with my heart. The long and short of it is that we made the decision that this was what we were to do. I said yes to what we understood the Lord was speaking. I only had one stipulation for the Lord. I told the Lord with humility yet boldness that if we were to move back to Waco, *I wanted my house back!* In my spirit I was ada-mant about it. I felt it was the justice of God that *I get my house back.* I wasn't speaking of the same house that some-one else now owned. I was speaking of the kind of house that would restore what had been lost and something that would equate again to being Mary's dream home.

I went before the Courts of Heaven and made my request before my Judge. Mary and I understood that it was His righteous judgment on our behalf that would pro-vide such a thing. In the natural, I didn't know how or if this could be done. We had come back into the bless-ing of God and had in fact seen God bring restoration to us financially, as a family, with our reputation and other areas. Yet to be able to see this kind of house be provided, I felt I needed a verdict of justice in my life from His Courts that would require the enemy to repay. This is exactly what happened. God blessed everything involved and we now live in a house that is *better* than the previous house. It is a result of the justice of God coming from the Courts of Heaven. We have seen and still see the restoring of God in our lives. We are living demonstrations of God's goodness and justice toward His elect.

Another thing we see from the story in Luke 18:1-8 is the issue of perseverance in the Courts. The widow would consistently and persistently present her case before the unjust Judge. Luke 18:5 shows the unjust Judge deciding to render a verdict on behalf of this woman because of her ongoing presentation of her case.

> Yet because this widow troubles me I will avenge her,
> lest by her continual coming she weary me.

This woman had no power, wealth, or ability to convince the judge to rule in her favor. The only thing she had at her disposal was a persistent presentation of her case. As a result of this the unjust judge decides that in spite of him not getting anything from it, he was going to render a judgment for her. This is the power of persistently petitioning the Courts of Heaven. Again, the moral of this story is *not* that God is an unjust Judge we must convince. The moral of the story is that if a widow with no power, wealth, or influence can convince an unjust judge to move on her behalf, how much more can we stand in the judicial system of Heaven and see our Judge rule for us. This is the power of persistence.

Sometimes people think that because they have made one attempt at coming into the Courts of Heaven everything should change. This isn't necessarily true. There are times when we must keep coming by faith and presenting our case and petitions before the Lord. As we do this, the Holy Spirit may reveal to us certain things we need to deal with that Satan is claiming to legally resist us. If we are persistently presenting our case, God can and will unveil the things that need to be moved that Satan would be using. This comes from a persistent presentation, perhaps over and over, of our petition and case before God. We are told in Hebrews 11:6 that God rewards faith and is a rewarder of those who seek Him fully.

> But without faith it is impossible to please Him, for he who comes to God must believe that He is, and that He is a rewarder of those who diligently seek Him.

People of real faith are people who diligently seek Him. They don't just try once and give up. They set their face like a flint and petition Him until the answer comes or the Holy Spirit reveals what is hindering it from coming.

As I was in Japan teaching on the Courts of Heaven, I had a very significant experience. I had a dream that revealed some necessary information that we needed to function in the Courts on behalf of the people and even the nation. This will happen to me frequently wherever I am ministering. God will give me a dream that will help me bring people into the Courts of Heaven and deal with things that would hinder breakthrough. In the dream I was standing in a house that wasn't mine. The people of the house were serving me a plate of food. I began to take a knife and fork and cut a piece of the food that was lying on the plate. As I cut it, I thought, *"That looks like a mouse."* I went ahead, however, and cut it and placed it in my mouth, but I thought *this is a mouse.* I then spit it out. I again cut another piece and did the same thing all over. It was like I was cutting the tail of the mouse and going about the process of *eating it,* even though I was spitting it out each time. As I finished cutting off what looked like the tail, I came to the *body* of the mouse. I then fully realized this *is a mouse.* I was appalled. I woke from the dream, thinking *this is crazy.* I had a sense, however, that it must be from the Lord. Who would dream such a thing? As the leaders of the ministry came and picked me up, I told them about the dream. We discussed and sought to see if it had any meaning or bearing on things. Then to my amazement the leader *found* a scripture in Isaiah 66:17 about *eating a mouse*. I thought, *"What?"*

> *"Those who sanctify themselves and purify*
> *themselves,*
> *To go to the gardens*
> *After an idol in the midst,*
> *Eating swine's flesh and the abomination and the*
> *mouse,*
> *Shall be consumed together,"* says the Lord.

Eating a mouse was the activity of those worshiping and serving an idol and a demon god. As we discussed this, we became aware it was a word to this group. That through compromises of small things that are thought to have no significance, we can actually be honoring and worshiping demon gods and granting them an authority over us. We knew there needed to be repentance to break any legal right ancient gods of Japan were claiming, because people were eating the mouse, and in doing so, making and empowering agreements with demon spirits. We dealt with this in the service and a great power and anointing resulted. This was done because this church and group are seeking God with all their hearts. They are constantly in the Courts presenting their case. Therefore, God saw fit to unveil something Satan would claim a legal right to use against them. When this was dealt with, another level of freedom and breakthrough came. This is because of a persistent presentation of their case in the Courts of Heaven. God is a rewarder of those who diligently seek Him. When we set our heart toward the Lord in persistent seeking, God is moved to unveil for us the hidden things so we can repent and deal with them. However, this comes at the expense of seeking Him diligently.

In the story Jesus told about the widow and the unjust judge Jesus says, "Hear what the unjust judge says." In other words, learn a lesson from his response to this woman who wouldn't stop. Jesus then makes this statement, "And will not God avenge His own elect who cry out to Him day and night? Yes, I say He will avenge them speedily." This portion of the story always confused me. It seems Jesus is speaking something paradoxical. He speaks of crying *day and night*, which would imply a long-term seeking of God. He also says, however, *"He will avenge them speedily."* I would think to myself, *so which is it?* Does it take a long time or do answers come quickly? Then one day it was as if God spoke to me. What I believe He showed me was that for those who have cried out *day and night* to the Lord, when they step into the Courts of Heaven their answers will come speedily. Their history with God grants them a place of influence and authority before the

Lord and His Courts. However, those who want to use the Courts of Heaven as a method or formula of prayer will probably get lesser results. Our time spent seeking the Lord is a weighty thing before Him. When we come before His Courts, this carries great influence in this dimension. The result can be quick and speedy results as we present our case in the judicial system of Heaven.

A final thought concerning insights about functioning in this Court is Jesus asked in Luke 18:8 if there would be faith in the earth when the Son of Man returned.

> *I tell you that He will avenge them speedily. Nevertheless, when the Son of Man comes, will He really find faith on the earth?*

Jesus declares that operating in the Courts of Heaven will cause God to avenge His people speedily. In other words, answers can come quickly. Jesus' question, however, was if this would cause faith to be in the earth, even though God was demonstrating His faithfulness to people. Faith or absolute trust in the character of God is birthed out of us witnessing and partaking of His faithfulness. This is what happened with Sarah after she had waited so long for a child. Hebrews 11:11 declares that Sarah came to the place where she *judged* God faithful.

*By faith Sarah herself also received strength to con-
ceive seed, and she bore a child when she was past
the age, because she judged Him faithful who had
promised.*

In other words, Sarah looked at all the evidence and
concluded that God was faithful and could be trusted. She
judged Him faithful. This brought faith that produced a
strength she conceived and gave birth from. Jesus is asking if there will be a people in the earth who see God's
faithfulness from His Courts and will allow a faith to arise
in their hearts. Or will they be an unbelieving people who
are yet to be convinced? God desires to show Himself so
faithful from the judicial system of Heaven that people
will be convinced of His character and power that can be
trusted. This was the trouble with the Israelites in their
wilderness journey. God led them through the wilderness
to perfect faith in them so they could cross over Jordan
and possess their inheritance. However, they saw the test
they went through not as something to equip them in their
faith but rather to destroy them. We are told that Jesus is
committed to perfecting our faith. Hebrews 12:2 shows us
that Jesus is the author and finisher of our faith.

*Looking unto Jesus, the author and finisher of our
faith, who for the joy that was set before Him endured*

> the cross, despising the shame, and has sat down at
> the right hand of the throne of God.

Jesus is dedicated to bringing our faith to full maturity and effectiveness. In fact, we see when the Son of Man returns, *faith* is what He will be looking for. Will He find it in His people? This is one of the main purposes in understanding and functioning in the Courts of Heaven. We are to operate in this realm and become convinced that God cannot lie. His word is true. He will accomplish in us, through us, and for us all He has promised.

This is what the first group of Israelites coming out of Egypt never got. When they went through the testing, instead of letting their faith develop, they rebelled and murmured against God and their God-given leaders. God finally had enough. Numbers 14:22-23 shows God testifying against them.

> Because all these men who have seen My glory and
> the signs which I did in Egypt and in the wilderness,
> and have put Me to the test now these ten times, and
> have not heeded My voice, they certainly shall not see
> the land of which I swore to their fathers, nor shall
> any of those who rejected Me see it.

God released a judgment against them that they would not get their inheritance. This was because the faithfulness of God never produced faith in them. They experienced and received the grace of God in vain (see Second Corinthians 6:1). In spite of God's faithfulness, their faith never developed. The intention of God was to lead them through the wilderness, show them His glory in every adverse situation they faced, and allow it to develop faith in them. They were then to have the necessary faith they needed by the time they came to crossing over into their promised land of inheritance. This didn't happen. Therefore, they were destined to wander in the wilderness for 40 years. God still took care of them, but they never got their inheritance. We must come to faith to be able to be willing to cross over when the time comes. Without it, we too will rebel and live an existence rather than a life of purpose.

The Court of Heaven is a place where we see the faithfulness of God. However, Jesus wanted to know—will it really birth faith in us, even though God *will* show Himself faithful? I hope and pray that I am and will become a man of faith who will not doubt God but will demonstrate faith in Him. That I will allow the answers that come from the Court of Heaven, God's judicial system, to so impact my life that faith erupts and bursts forth from me. The bottom line is: God is and will be faithful from His judicial system. However, will we judge Him to be faithful? Will we allow the faithfulness of God from His Courts to prove His heart toward us? Grant it to be so, Lord!

Lord, as I stand before Your Courts, I ask for Your grace to function in and from this place. My cry, Lord, is for decisions rendered that would allow me to prosper because of what You have done for me on the cross. Would you reveal, Lord, anything the devil would be contending before Your Courts that would be denying me the right to wealth and prosperity? As I understand this, Lord, I purpose to repent and agree with Your word and activity on my behalf. My desire, Lord, is to see prosperity come for me, my family, and Your kingdom purposes. I ask, Lord, for a decision of justice to be rendered in my life from Your Courts. Would You allow justice to flow like a river and bring all forms of restoration to me including prosperity and wealth. Lord, I ask and desire for Your will to be done on earth just as it is in Heaven. In Jesus' Name, amen.

CHAPTER 3

CONTENDING TO BIRTH WEALTH

We are told clearly in God's Word that wealth is necessary to the purposes of God. Deuteronomy 8:18 is a very clear statement of this.

And you shall remember the Lord your God, for it is He who gives you power to get wealth, that He may establish His covenant which He swore to your fathers, as it is this day.

If God's covenant purposes are to be done in the earth and His government and kingdom are to expand, wealth is a necessity. This scripture could not be any clearer. God grants the power to get wealth so His will and purposes can be done. Without wealth the intent and desire of God will be frustrated and even forfeited.

I remember years ago hearing a preacher/teacher from a certain movement give a definition of prosperity. He said, "Prosperity is never having to tell God 'no' again." He then shared that when tragedy would strike a place in the form of tornadoes, floods, earthquake, or other devastating circumstances, he and his wife had such resources that they *personally* would send 18-wheel trucks full of provision for the people suffering. He didn't have to send it through agencies who took large portions of the donations for "administrative costs" or other organization expenses. They could, from their own wealth, get the needed things into the hands of the people quickly and effectively. In other words, they knew what God's heart would be in matters such as these, and they could meet the need because of their wealth. This is what he meant by not having to tell God "No." They were able to demonstrate the love of God to these in the Name of Jesus because of the wealth they had accumulated.

When I heard this, it brought a new perspective to me about wealth, riches, and prosperity. If we are going to manifest the love of Jesus and see God's heart revealed in nations, it will take massive amounts of wealth. This wealth is not just about being benevolent to those in need. This wealth is about releasing influence that unveils the ways of God and His heart to a culture. We have all sorts of philosophies being espoused today. Many of them are being driven by the Anti-Christ spirit that is seeking to control and rule the cultures of nations. The problem is those who carry these ideas have the money to get these concepts embedded in societies. If we as the church and God's people are going to contend for the culture of nations, we will also have to have the resources to compete. This means God's promise of giving us the *power to get wealth* must be realized. The issue here is that it seems that the devil's people have the money. Why is this? Why is it that God's people are not the wealthy ones with the influence riches carry? The answer is there are judicial cases the devil has filed against us in the Courts of Heaven that are stopping us from prospering on that level.

It is no mistake that Abraham, Isaac, and Jacob's wives were all barren. Sarah, Rebekah, and Rachel all could not have children. Yet the line of Ishmael grew and increased exponentially. Remember that Abraham asked God to allow Ishmael to be the *promised one*. However, God said no! Genesis 17:18-19 tells us that even though Sarah was barren, God chose her womb to be the one for the *seed* to come through.

> And Abraham said to God, "Oh, that Ishmael might live before You!"
>
> Then God said: "No, Sarah your wife shall bear you a son, and you shall call his name Isaac; I will establish My covenant with him for an everlasting covenant, and with his descendants after him."

Isaac would be the one through whom the *kingdom seed* would come. God's plans to redeem the earth and mankind would come through Isaac. The principle is this. Anything that has a heart for the kingdom of God, the devil will resist with barrenness. There will be an inability to be fruitful that will harass this people. It will be necessary to figure out why the barrenness is there and how to remove it so blessing, fruitfulness, and prosperity can occur.

This is why so many people are frustrated. They have a desire, sense, word, and promise that they are to prosper. Yet it seems like it goes the other way. This is because the devil has discovered something legal against them to stop their prosperity and produce barrenness. Remember that First Peter 5:8 tells us *our adversary* (legal opponent) is seeking to devour us. He is endeavoring through legal means in the spirit to devour the prosperity we are to walk in. He is seeking to stop the *birthing* of wealth. Only when we deal with this legal issue in the Courts of Heaven will we see the fullness of the desire come. Satan's attempts in these areas are to stop the purposes of the kingdom of God. Wealth is so God's covenant purposes might be established. We get blessed in the process of seeing this wealth manifest.

We are told in Deuteronomy 8:18 that we can receive *power to get wealth*. The word *get* in the Hebrew is *asah*. It can mean several things. It is also used in Genesis 1:11.

> *Then God said, "Let the earth bring forth grass, the*
> *herb that yields seed, and the fruit tree that yields*
> *fruit according to its kind, whose seed is in itself, on*
> *the earth"; and it was so.*

In this verse the word *yields* is the word *asah*. It implies that which is produced or brought forth. It is that which comes from a *seed*. Everything God does starts with a seed. Even a child being conceived is the result of a *seed*. When a man impregnates a woman, it is done through his *seed*. When God impregnates us with the favor, an idea, wisdom, or concepts, it is Him putting His seed in us. We become His womb to bring forth or yield a harvest from the seed He has deposited in us. The *power to get wealth* is from a seed in us. It is something we conceive and carry to full term. We have to steward the seed to see it produce abundantly. Many people are waiting for God to *give* them wealth. God doesn't *give* wealth. He *gives* the power to get wealth. We have to take the *seed of power* and produce wealth with it. This comes out of the creativity, wisdom, and discernment of God. Jeremiah 17:5-6 tells us that those who have their confidence in the flesh will not recognize the opportunities given them from God to produce wealth.

> *Thus says the Lord:*
> *"Cursed is the man who trusts in man*

And makes flesh his strength,

Whose heart departs from the Lord.

For he shall be like a shrub in the desert,

And shall not see when good comes,

But shall inhabit the parched places in the wilderness,

In a salt land which is not inhabited."

He will not see when good comes. When we have our confidence alone in what we can do from our own abilities, we miss moments in God. We must always look at things through God's eyes and abilities. When we trust only in our own ability and our heart is not depending on God, we become like a shrub in the desert. We inhabit parched and dry places rather than lush, fruitful, and prosperous places. This is because we could be *looking* for wealth rather than the *power* to get wealth. Remember, God wants to deposit a seed in us. An idea, favor, creativity, or wisdom that when handled correctly can produce and yield a bountiful harvest.

This is what Peter almost missed when Jesus got into his boat in Luke 5:4-8.

When He had stopped speaking, He said to Simon, "Launch out into the deep and let down your nets for a catch."

But Simon answered and said to Him, "Master, we have toiled all night and caught nothing; nevertheless at Your word I will let down the net." And when they had done this, they caught a great number of fish, and their net was breaking. So they signaled to their partners in the other boat to come and help them. And they came and filled both the boats, so that they began to sink. When Simon Peter saw it, he fell down at Jesus' knees, saying, "Depart from me, for I am a sinful man, O Lord!"

Peter argued and doubted that Jesus knew what He was talking about. Peter's present experience said there were no fish out there. Yet Jesus is telling him to launch out and let down his *nets*. Notice Jesus told Peter to let down *nets*, but Peter only let down a *net*. This is why it broke. Peter's lack of faith in fully obeying Jesus cost him an even bigger catch. He allowed his own natural man and his confidence and trust in the flesh (his experience as a fisherman), more than the word of God, to cause him to miss a moment. He forfeited a major part of his *power to get wealth*.

Don't think of these *fish* as *souls of men*. We can tend to over-spiritualize this event and miss what God wants us to see. Peter was a fisherman. He made his living by the fish he caught. This kind of catch that would have occurred had he fully obeyed and not trusted in the flesh could have made him a wealthy man. However, Peter missed the moment and the opportunity being presented to him. Being willing to fully believe and obey is critical to operating in the power to get wealth. When God trusts us with an idea, concept, favor, or wisdom, we must move in faith with it. Otherwise we can lose an opportunity from the Lord.

In the midst of any barrenness, we must contend for our harvest and for wealth. We have established that it is God's heart and even need for us to be wealthy. What He intends to do in the earth must involve wealthy people. We have also established that the devil fights fruitfulness, prosperity, and riches in those who are of a kingdom heart and expression. He knows if we step into the realm of wealth appointed to us, he will see his desire revoked. It is to his advantage to keep us in lack, need, and poverty. This is why so many good, well-meaning, and faithful people have never been able to see prosperity.

We see this whole barrenness issue in Jacob's wife, Rachel. Rachel was barren and unable to conceive. For the sake of our analogy, she couldn't conceive wealth and bring it forth. We see that she then resorts to giving Jacob her handmaiden to bear children for her. This seems to be a practice in those days for barren women. The handmaiden does indeed become pregnant and brings forth a son. Rachel herself will later bear children as well.

However, when this child by the handmaiden is born, Rachel declares something very powerful. Genesis 30:6 records Rachel's declaration at the boy's birth.

> *Then Rachel said, "God has judged my case; and He has also heard my voice and given me a son." Therefore she called his name Dan.*

Rachel proclaims, "*God has judged my case.*" Rachel understood that barrenness had begun to be broken off her and what was joined to her. God had heard her voice and started to produce fruitfulness for her and through her. She was so convinced of this that she called the boy "Dan." Dan means *judge* in the Hebrew. He would be an ever-present reminder that Courtroom activity had transpired on her behalf and barrenness had been removed from her situation. God had heard Rachel's cry and had judged for her. The reproach of barrenness was being lifted. Barrenness on any level brings a reproach. When we are unable to conceive and produce, it results in frustration, shame, and sorrow. However, when the sting of barrenness is lifted and blessings begin to come, there is a sense of justification, vindication, and joy. This is true on every level but especially where it relates to wealth, riches, and prosperity.

I have a friend who had a dream where he saw a lot of people pregnant but unable to give birth. He said in the dream that some had been pregnant for nine months and should be getting ready to give birth. Others had been pregnant for over a year. Still others were pregnant for five and even ten years. They were carrying something in their womb but unable to bring it forth. He knew in the dream the reason why they couldn't give birth was legal accusations against them. As a result, they were perpetually pregnant with no hope of seeing what they carried actually come into reality. The devil will seek to stop us from birthing wealth through accusation against us. Perhaps we haven't been able to *conceive*. Maybe we have *conceived* but can't seem to bring forth. The accusation of the devil as our legal opponent will keep what we are carrying from actually manifesting. Maybe he stops the right people from favoring you. Perhaps he hinders money that would be necessary to get the project off the ground. He might mess with scheduling and timing. Whatever and however he does it, he hinders the birthing of wealth into the earth through God's kingdom people. We must know how to see Satan's legal rights revoked and wealth be born and produced in the earth. This will end barrenness in the people of God and unlock the intentions of the Lord through His people.

One more thing I would point out about contending for wealth. In Deuteronomy 8:18 the promise to get wealth was given to the *fathers*. This means the accumulation of wealth is a generational issue. So often we think of only what we can gather in just our own lifetime. However, to see wealth stewarded and accumulated on a massive scale can require succeeding generations and their stewardship. This will mandate that those who come after us carry good business sense and a value system that allows increase to wealth. It is a proven fact that most *family* businesses go bankrupt in the third generation. This is because by that time the people in charge of the money have no awareness of the process it took to produce what they now oversee. The result is a lack of a value for it and quite often a squandering of the wealth rather than an increasing of it. The solution to this is to educate those who will care for the wealth so that it is increased and not diminished.

The other issue concerning accumulating wealth over successive generations is it takes the pressure off just one generation. For instance, perhaps I do not have enough years to accumulate wealth on a significant level. I can, however, accumulate as much as I can and hand it to the next generation to steward. This gets the ball rolling so to speak. I can impregnate the coming generation with a value system and skill set that would be necessary to increase wealth and riches so the kingdom of God can be financed. This way each of us can be a part of the wealth transfer that will allow the work of God to prosper and flourish for decades and centuries to come.

We must fight and contend for wealth to be birthed. As we do, we can see the plans, desires, longings, and intentions of the Lord done. We can overcome barrenness and bring forth fruitfully. In the next chapters, we will discuss some of the issues to target to remove the legal rights of the devil. The result will be prosperity on new levels.

> Lord, as I come before Your Courts, I ask that all rights of barrenness and unfruitfulness to operate against me would be revoked. I ask that prosperity would be sent into my life as a part of Your kingdom seed. Let every attempt of the devil to set reproach in my life through unfruitfulness, even in the financial realm, be annulled. Allow every right he is claiming to be answered by the blood of Jesus speaking on my behalf. Lord, I say that even as Sarah, Rachel, and Rebekah came out of barrenness and into fruitfulness, so do I as one set by You. I decree that I am free to prosper and increase for Your kingdom purpose and intent in Jesus' Name, amen.

CHAPTER 4

THE GREAT
WEALTH TRANSFER

Most of us believe that God has promised in His Word, both through principle and example, a great wealth transfer. What is meant by this statement is that we are confident that instead of the wicked possessing the wealth of the world, God's people will become the possessors of it. The reason for this transaction would be for the purpose of transformation of the nations and not just personal material blessings. I want to make it abundantly clear that I believe God has no problem with us personally prospering. The Bible is clear concerning this. Psalm 35:27 literally states that God has pleasure and delight in our prosperity and wellbeing.

Let them shout for joy and be glad,
Who favor my righteous cause;
And let them say continually,

"Let the Lord be magnified,

Who has pleasure in the prosperity of His servant."

God has no delight in His servants living in lack, need, and poverty. On the other hand, He is excited and blessed when we are prosperous and enlarged. First Timothy 6:17 tells us that God actually gives us *things* to enjoy. The idea that God is some kind of miser who doesn't want us to have anything in this life is completely against scripture. It is, in fact, the idea propagated by a religious spirit that is painting a wrong concept of who God is.

Command those who are rich in this present age not
to be haughty, nor to trust in uncertain riches but in
the living God, who gives us richly all things to enjoy.

When we are blessed and trusted with wealth and riches, we are to use them wisely and not trust in them. Our confidence should never be in anything but God Himself. However, when we have allowed God to work in our lives so we can righteously steward riches and prosperity, He will trust us with it. We will be allowed to enjoy it, all the while thanking Him and glorifying Him for His goodness in our lives. This process that God takes some through to prepare them for wealth, riches, and prosperity can be found in Deuteronomy 8:1-9.

Every commandment which I command you today you must be careful to observe, that you may live and multiply, and go in and possess the land of which the Lord swore to your fathers. And you shall remember that the Lord your God led you all the way these forty years in the wilderness, to humble you and test you, to know what was in your heart, whether you would keep His commandments or not. So He humbled you, allowed you to hunger, and fed you with manna which you did not know nor did your fathers know, that He might make you know that man shall not live by bread alone; but man lives by every word that proceeds from the mouth of the Lord. Your garments did not wear out on you, nor did your foot swell these forty years. You should know in your heart that as a man chastens his son, so the Lord your God chastens you.

Therefore you shall keep the commandments of the Lord your God, to walk in His ways and to fear Him. For the Lord your God is bringing you into a good land, a land of brooks of water, of fountains and springs, that flow out of valleys and hills; a land of wheat and barley, of vines and fig trees and pome-granates, a land of olive oil and honey; a land in which you will eat bread without scarcity, in which

you will lack nothing; a land whose stones are iron
and out of whose hills you can dig copper.

Notice that the Lord allowed them to hunger, yet supernaturally supplied for them. He wanted them to have their confidence in Him and not the stuff. He tested their hearts and transformed them into people who would live by the word they heard from Him. He wanted them to enjoy the provisions without letting it capture them. Once this process was complete, He brought them into the land of abundance. Notice it was a land without scarcity and where they would lack nothing! The problem is that many never allow this process to be worked in their lives so God can trust them with wealth. They never learn to *live by every word that proceeds from the mouth of God.* In other words, they draw life out of the God they are experiencing in their heart and not just what they have in their hand. When God has established in us a love for Him and an excitement about who He is and what He speaks, then He can trust us with wealth.

Mary and I walked through this process. We struggled for at least a couple of decades in our marriage. True, over that time we had six children and that requires a lot of money. However, through that period of *not enough*, something happened in our lives. We learned to live by every word that proceeded from the mouth of God. I spent much time in prayer petitioning the Lord to please meet our needs. I asked for money to keep the electricity on. I asked for money to keep the water and gas on. I asked for money to keep them from repossessing our house. I asked for money to not lose the car to creditors. Lest you think I am exaggerating, think again. These were hard times when our only dependence was on God.

You also need to know that I wasn't sitting around not working. There were times I had three jobs at one time. I cleaned houses and mowed yards in addition to working a full-time job. I was the janitor at the church, which brought in some additional finances. When I went on full-time staff as a pastor, I then delivered newspapers every afternoon and early in the morning (like 3-4 AM). I would do this, then go and teach the class at 9 AM on Sunday mornings; that was my responsibility. Then I would spend all day at the church getting ready after the morning service to preach on Sunday evening. I worked hard! Yet we were barely surviving. But we survived. God allowed us to hunger, but fed us. We learned how to draw our life from Him and have our full confidence in Him. We learned how to use our faith and believe Him when everything seemed to be crashing in.

Through *all* these times He was faithful. Somewhere along the way, *we passed the test!* Prosperity began to come. Blessing began to arise. We started to accumulate. Then I discovered if you have something God blessed you with, someone will try and take it away. This is what they did, because of my naïveté. As a result of me not paying close enough attention to a warning from God in a couple of dreams, some people stole away what God had blessed and trusted us with. I spent many years repenting and asking God to forgive while I also forgave those who did this to us. God blessed us again. Today we have seen the restoration of God. We are living a life of eating bread with no scarcity. We are enjoying the good things of God. This is because we allowed the Lord to work His process in us so we could be trusted with wealth and lack nothing.

Having said all of this, we should also know that wealth, riches, and prosperity are to be used for kingdom purposes. God does want us blessed as individuals and families. However, the kingdom purpose of wealth is to expand God's rule in the earth. We saw in Deuteronomy 8:18 this reality.

> And you shall remember the Lord your God, for it is He who gives you power to get wealth, that He may establish His covenant which He swore to your fathers, as it is this day.

Wealth is for the purpose of seeing the covenant of God established. His covenant involves the redemption and reclaiming of the nations of the earth. This requires great finances. These finances will come through His people. One of the things the Bible teaches is these finances will be the result of a great wealth transfer. Several scriptures speak of this. Proverbs 13:22 promises that the sinner's wealth will be entrusted to the righteous.

> *A good man leaves an inheritance to his children's children,*
>
> *But the wealth of the sinner is stored up for the righteous.*

God declares that what the sinner accumulates will be ultimately given to the hand of the righteous. This is because wealth grants influence and power. When the wicked have the wealth, they therefore have the influence. We see this every day in our society. We see the godless agenda of these wealthy people being pushed. However, God says that He will see to it that the wealth that grants this impact will be taken from them and given to the righteous. The righteous will then be the ones who have the influence. They can then promote the agendas of Heaven rather than of hell. This cannot happen without a transfer of wealth. Ecclesiastes 2:26 also speaks of this wealth transfer.

> *For God gives wisdom and knowledge and joy to a man who is good in His sight; but to the sinner He*

gives the work of gathering and collecting, that he may give to him who is good before God. This also is vanity and grasping for the wind.

It seems that God is in the business of redistributing wealth. He takes it from the sinner, who He uses to collect it. He then gives it to the one who is good in His sight. When it says *in His sight*, I esteem that to mean that God has pondered and investigated these lives to see if they qualify to handle His wealth. Remember that God claims all wealth for Himself in Haggai 2:8.

"The silver is Mine, and the gold is Mine," says the Lord of hosts.

As all the wealth is God's, He gives it to whomever He will. He grants it to the ones He esteems are good in His sight. When we pass the scrutiny of God, we can then be entrusted with the transfer of wealth that is not just for us, but ultimately for God's intent in the nations. This scrutiny will be used to prepare us to care for that which is precious to the Lord.

Let me mention three places in scripture where we see a wealth transfer occur. These places can help us discern some of the principles that govern this. The first one I will mention is when Israel came out of Egypt. Exodus 12:33-36 tells us that the Jews plundered the Egyptians.

*And the Egyptians urged the people, that they might
send them out of the land in haste. For they said, "We
shall all be dead." So the people took their dough
before it was leavened, having their kneading bowls
bound up in their clothes on their shoulders. Now
the children of Israel had done according to the word
of Moses, and they had asked from the Egyptians
articles of silver, articles of gold, and clothing. And
the Lord had given the people favor in the sight of
the Egyptians, so that they granted them what they
requested. Thus they plundered the Egyptians.*

The Egyptians, it seemed, were so anxious for the
Israelites to leave because of all the plagues they had experienced that they gave them whatever they wanted. When
the Jews left Egypt, they took the wealth of Egypt with
them. God transferred the wealth of Egypt into the hands
of Israel. This happened because God gave them extreme
favor in the sight of the Egyptians. Psalm 105:37 declares
that the once band of slaves now possessed the gold and
silver of Egypt.

> *He also brought them out with silver and gold,*
> *And there was none feeble among His tribes.*

Only God could orchestrate such a thing. Some, of
which I would be one, believe that God gave Israel the

back wages that were theirs for being slaves for 400-plus years. He repaid them in a night for all the suffering, toil, and affliction that had been laid on them for centuries. God is a God of justice and will render it on our behalf.

A second place I see a wealth transfer is with Jacob. Laban had also sought to cheat and swindle his son-in-law who worked for him. He had changed his wages ten times to try and prohibit him from prospering too much. When Jacob confronts him about this, Laban is forced to make a deal with Jacob to try and keep him with him. Laban recognized the blessing he was experiencing because of the blessing that was on Jacob. Genesis 30:27 records Laban admitting that God blessed him because of Jacob.

> And Laban said to him, "Please stay, if I have found favor in your eyes, for I have learned by experience that the Lord has blessed me for your sake."

Jacob agrees to stay but only on his terms. Genesis 30:31-43 shows this whole scenario playing out.

> So he said, "What shall I give you?"
>
> And Jacob said, "You shall not give me anything. If you will do this thing for me, I will again feed and keep your flocks: Let me pass through all your flock today, removing from there all the speckled and spotted sheep, and all the brown ones among the lambs,

and the spotted and speckled among the goats; and these shall be my wages. So my righteousness will answer for me in time to come, when the subject of my wages comes before you: every one that is not speckled and spotted among the goats, and brown among the lambs, will be considered stolen, if it is with me."

And Laban said, "Oh, that it were according to your word!" So he removed that day the male goats that were speckled and spotted, all the female goats that were speckled and spotted, every one that had some white in it, and all the brown ones among the lambs, and gave them into the hand of his sons. Then he put three days' journey between himself and Jacob, and Jacob fed the rest of Laban's flocks.

Now Jacob took for himself rods of green poplar and of the almond and chestnut trees, peeled white strips in them, and exposed the white which was in the rods. And the rods which he had peeled, he set before the flocks in the gutters, in the watering troughs where the flocks came to drink, so that they should conceive when they came to drink. So the flocks conceived before the rods, and the flocks brought forth streaked, speckled, and spotted. Then Jacob separated the lambs, and made the flocks face toward the streaked and all the brown in the flock of Laban; but he put

> *his own flocks by themselves and did not put them with Laban's flock.*
>
> *And it came to pass, whenever the stronger livestock conceived, that Jacob placed the rods before the eyes of the livestock in the gutters, that they might conceive among the rods. But when the flocks were feeble, he did not put them in; so the feebler were Laban's and the stronger Jacob's. Thus the man became exceedingly prosperous, and had large flocks, female and male servants, and camels and donkeys.*

I'm not really sure of the science/biology behind what Jacob did. All I know is that through a wisdom he had, he took away what he had lost from Laban and gained it back for himself. This happened so much that in Genesis 31:1 the sons of Laban recognized there had been a wealth transfer.

> *Now Jacob heard the words of Laban's sons, saying, "Jacob has taken away all that was our father's, and from what was our father's he has acquired all this wealth."*

This wealth transfer occurred because of wisdom that Jacob had. Wisdom is simply the ability to see what others are missing. People who prosper greatly are those who are able to recognize a trend, pattern, or timing of where things are. When this is realized and taken advantage of, great wealth can be the result. They see when to invest, when to buy, when to sell. They can see a trend coming that they move to take advantage of. They are able to see when *good comes*. As we saw before, but it bears repeating, this is what Jeremiah 17:5-6 is alluding to. It is declaring that when we only look and have confidence in the flesh, we miss opportunities because we don't see them.

> *Thus says the Lord:*
> *"Cursed is the man who trusts in man*
> *And makes flesh his strength,*
> *Whose heart departs from the Lord.*
> *For he shall be like a shrub in the desert,*
> *And shall not see when good comes,*
> *But shall inhabit the parched places in the wilderness,*
> *In a salt land which is not inhabited."*

We must be able to see the opportunities that are before us that others are missing. This is what Jacob did. The result was a transfer of wealth into his hands. How many times has God granted us ideas, concepts, insight, and/or connections and we squandered them away because we really didn't *see* them. We must learn to walk circumspectly and not miss the things God is unveiling to us. Hebrews

4:1 exhorts us to fear lest we miss out on something God has for us.

> *Therefore, since a promise remains of entering His rest, let us fear lest any of you seem to have come short of it.*

My prayer is, "O God, help me to see and not miss what You would have for me." I do not want to come up short of something God intended to do for me and through me for His purposes in the earth.

The third place I see a wealth transfer is with Peter and the catch of fish Jesus intended for him in Luke 5:4-11. Jesus challenged Peter to launch out and let down his nets, plural. When you look at this scripture the Bible says he let down a net, singular.

> *When He had stopped speaking, He said to Simon, "Launch out into the deep and let down your nets for a catch."*
>
> *But Simon answered and said to Him, "Master, we have toiled all night and caught nothing; nevertheless at Your word I will let down the net." And when they had done this, they caught a great number of fish, and their net was breaking. So they signaled to their partners in the other boat to come and help them. And they came and filled both the boats, so*

that they began to sink. When Simon Peter saw it, he fell down at Jesus' knees, saying, "Depart from me, for I am a sinful man, O Lord!"

For he and all who were with him were astonished at the catch of fish which they had taken; and so also were James and John, the sons of Zebedee, who were partners with Simon. And Jesus said to Simon, "Do not be afraid. From now on you will catch men." So when they had brought their boats to land, they forsook all and followed Him.

Peter, it seems, was just humoring Jesus. He did not expect any kind of a catch. As a result of this lack of faith in Jesus and His word, it says he would let down a *net*. To his and everyone else's astonishment the catch was so great the *net* broke. This was because Jesus was releasing *nets* of fish, not *a net* of fish. Peter at this moment was brought to the end of himself as his unbelieving, evil heart was manifested. Hebrews 3:12 exhorts us not to have an *evil* heart of unbelief.

Beware, brethren, lest there be in any of you an evil heart of unbelief in departing from the living God.

Unbelief is not to be tolerated as part of our humanity. We are not to make excuses for it. We are to repent of it as an evil thing before God. This is what is happening to

Peter. The catch of fish he has just experienced pierced his heart and shattered his natural confidence. He was impacted with an awareness of who Jesus is. He realized he missed an appointed time. Jesus would have granted to Peter enough money and finances through this transfer of wealth into his hands to care for him and his family as he potentially followed Jesus. Please do not over-spiritualize what happened in this story. Fish in this story do not represent souls. Fish in this story represent money. These fish would have been taken to market, sold, and the wealth would have made Peter rich, affluent, and prosperous. God would have put into his hands riches. The main key in this story is to hear God and do what He says no matter how ludicrous it seems. Peter had fished all night and caught nothing. Yet Jesus knew by supernatural means the fish that were there or would be there. If Peter had been able to lay aside his natural logic and just by faith believe, the results would have been phenomenal.

So they can be for us as well. It's not that we lay aside natural logic. No, God has given us minds to think and reason with. We do, however, lay that down when we hear the word of the Lord. His voice trumps our logic, intellect, and experience. When we hear Him, we must obey. This can produce a wealth transfer in our hands for our blessing and the increase of His government in the earth.

Lord, as I stand in Your Courts, I petition You for the great wealth transfer that is promised in Your Word. I believe, Lord, that You cause all things to come to order for the blessing of God to overtake me in Jesus' Name. Lord, I ask that there would be a removing of wealth from those who would use it against Your will and purpose in the earth. I also ask that there would be a trusting of this wealth to the righteous who would use it in agreement with Your will. Lord, may I be found as one who can be entrusted with Your silver and gold that would empower Your passion. Open my heart to Your ways and make me discerning that I might be used of You to steward the wealth of God in and through my life. Lord, I yield myself to You and ask for decisions to be rendered from Your Court that will produce this wealth transfer, in Jesus' Name.

CHAPTER 5

REVOKING THE POVERTY SPIRIT

One of the main enemies working against our prosperity in the spirit realm is the poverty spirit. I choose this term strategically in agreement with the scriptures to describe this foe. If we are to prosper, we must see the legal rights of this spiritual adversary annulled. Proverbs 6:9-11 gives us some necessary insight in combatting this spirit in the legal realms of the spirit world.

How long will you slumber, O sluggard?

When will you rise from your sleep?

A little sleep, a little slumber,

A little folding of the hands to sleep—

So shall your poverty come on you like a prowler,

And your need like an armed man.

First of all, notice that this verse declares *"your poverty"* will come on you. I was in Zimbabwe ministering in a very powerful church. The pastor had asked me if I could teach on how to shift the economy of a culture from a Court of Heaven perspective. I was excited to take on this challenge and seek to bring some enlightenment to this idea. As I stood to teach, I read this scripture. As I did it seemed as if this verse, and in particular these words, *jumped off the page* at me. I had never *seen* the *"your"* in this scripture before. I had always just thought about poverty coming to attack us. However, I am now *seeing* the *"your"* with new eyes from this scripture.

As these words from this verse leapt from the page, the Holy Spirit whispered in my ears, "There is a poverty spirit *assigned* to you [not just me but many, if not all]. If you get into agreement with it, it will claim you and your generations. This will empower it and it will consume and devour your life and the lives of your lineage." *Wow!* This was a completely new thought to me. The poverty spirit owns me because it claims me based on my agreement with it. It is *mine or yours* as the scripture said. In these verses the thing that puts us in agreement with the poverty spirit is laziness and lack of diligence. There are other things that can bring us into agreement with it as well. We will look at some of these also. Now, however, let's seek to get some more understanding of this thing called *poverty* that is assigned to us.

The first thing we should know is that being unfaithful and not taking care of business doesn't just produce natural circumstances. It actually can bring an agreement with a poverty spirit. What starts off as natural activity can produce in us a demonic control that takes ownership of our lives and seeks to fashion our future. This can be deadly and dangerous from a perspective of forfeiting our God-ordained future. For instance, we would think laziness is just an activity that can produce want and need because we don't take care of our business of being a worker and an enterprising person. This does happen. We are being warned, however, that if we do this enough, even just a little, poverty, which is a spirit, will come and take over our lives and future.

This scripture seems to emphasize being lazy just a *little*. In other words, it doesn't take long to grant the spirit of poverty the legal right to consume. It speaks of a *little* sleep, *a little* slumber, and a *little* folding of the hands. It seems that the three things mentioned here are progressive in nature. In other words, one thing allowed produces the next until the spirit of poverty now is controlling our lives. The word *sleep* is the Hebrew word *shehah*. It means "to be slack." It also is the idea of growing old. In other words, there is no energy or vitality. There is no diligence or driving force left in a person. Growing or being old speaks of no vision and dream for the future. *Old* has nothing to do with age. *Old* is a mindset and perspective. If we let this develop in our lives, we are setting ourselves up for poverty. A *little* of this will welcome poverty into our lives.

This verse also speaks of a *little* slumber. It is the Hebrew word *tnuwmah.* It means drowsiness. If we *let* ourselves grow old with no dream or future, *drowsiness* will come on us. This speaks of depression and no motivation. We have no reason to get out of bed in the morning. There is nothing to capture our hearts and make us excited about life. We must not allow this to conquer us or possess us. This process will invite the poverty assigned to us to overtake us. Now we are not just reaping our time of lack of diligence—now a spirit of poverty is determining our destiny and future.

The third thing mentioned that brings *your poverty* is a folding of the hands. This Hebrew word is *chibbug.* It means "a clasping of the hands in idleness." The idea is that we are not involving our hands in activity and enterprise that could produce wealth, prosperity, and riches for us. Our hands are idle. I remember working for a local city early in my work life right after I graduated from high school. Mary and I were a young married couple and I was feeling the responsibility to provide for us. It didn't pay very much, but as an uneducated person at the time it was all I was qualified for. I had been raised by my parents to be a worker. Laziness was not tolerated in the home I grew up in. This means that there was *put* into me a work ethic. I understood if I was to have something, I had to produce it myself. I am thankful for that until this day.

On this first job I had, the supervisor whom I worked under would not allow any of us to put our hands in our pockets. Even if we were standing waiting for something, we had to keep our hands out of our pockets. This might seem foolish today. Yet this older man understood something. Hands in the pocket demonstrated an attitude that wasn't consistent with diligence and ingenuity. He wanted the work force he was responsible for to not be lazy and in fact to be energetic. He knew that placing our hands in our pockets did not breed in us a worker's mentality. We were in fact clasping our hands together in idleness. Even if the moment we were in did not demand physical activity, he wanted us mentally ready to work! This is so very important. Many find themselves without this mentality bred into them. They are content to stand idly by rather than to be enterprising and moving with initiative. The problem with this is it can invite the poverty spirit assigned to you to come after you and your future.

Notice that *poverty* isn't a condition. It is pictured as a *prowler and an armed man*. A prowler is one who steals while an armed man is one who is empowered with strength against us. This means *poverty* is a spiritual entity and personality. When we are dealing with this spirit, we are not combatting a condition; we are seeking to annul the rights of a demonic being that has claimed a right to devour us. The Hebrew word for *prowler* is *halak*. It means "to walk." The idea is this spirit that desires to take over our lives is walking about searching and looking for an opportunity to devour. This is always the nature of the devil. He is always *walking to and fro and back and forwards* (see Job 1:6; I Peter 5:8). These terms imply he is seeking out and searching for any legal right he can find to devour and steal from us. This is what poverty does. The *armed man* is the Hebrew word *magen*. It means "a shield." It also speaks of the scaly hide of a crocodile. Of course, the crocodile is a devourer. It is telling us that poverty is something that is powerful and not easily dealt with. In its efforts to devour us it is a protected and shielded enemy. This means we should guard ourselves meticulously from giving this thing any advantage over us. Second Corinthians 2:11 warns us to not be ignorant of the ways the enemy employs.

> *Lest Satan should take advantage of us; for we are not ignorant of his devices.*

Ignorance is a great helper of the devil and his hordes. Through our ignorance he gets an advantage of us. The best thing is to never allow this by becoming wise to his ways. However, if we have fallen prey to this spirit of poverty assigned to us, we *can* get free from its influence and even dominance over our lives that is prohibiting our prosperity. However, if *the armed man* has come upon us we must take away the armor in which he trusts. This is what Jesus said in Luke 11:21-22:

> *When a strong man, fully armed, guards his own palace, his goods are in peace. But when a stronger than he comes upon him and overcomes him, he takes from him all his armor in which he trusted, and divides his spoils.*

Sometimes the taking away of the armor that the strong man trusts in is a process. We must stand before the Courts of Heaven and methodically revoke the legal right this enemy is claiming to devour our prosperity. We have looked at laziness and being given to a lack of diligence as one of the things that places us legally in agreement with the prowler/armed man of poverty. There are, however, other issues that can empower this spirit that desires to claim us and our family line. We can never prosper if this spirit legally has control of us and our future.

Poverty finds a right to legally possess when we refuse correction and instruction. Proverbs 13:18 declares lack and shame come from this spirit's influence.

Poverty and shame will come to him who disdains correction,

But he who regards a rebuke will be honored.

Having a *know-it-all* attitude will cause poverty and shame to possess us. The remedy for this is the fear of the Lord. We must walk in the fear of the Lord and realize that God will chasten us and correct us. He does this because of His great love for us (see Hebrews 12:6). If we refuse this correction, we will reap the consequences of our arrogance. We must repent, sometimes, of not repenting. I have found that the Lord will set boundaries that I am not to cross. If I do, I can step into territories where the enemy has legal access to me. God's correction will keep me from these places if I will pay attention to His correction and walk in the fear of the Lord.

Another thing that grants our poverty access is addictive behavior. Proverbs 23:21 tells us that allowing the craving of our flesh to rule can bring poverty.

For the drunkard and the glutton will come to poverty,

And drowsiness will clothe a man with rags.

When we allow addiction to control our lives, it can grant access to the spirit of poverty. This can be true for us individually. However, if there is a history of alcoholism, drug addiction, sexual issues, and other realms of the flesh out of control in our ancestry, this can have allowed the poverty spirit to claim a bloodline and its lineage. This will cause poverty to become a generational issue. You may look back at your family and see only poverty. This is because of a right someone gave to the devil in your family that allows him to visit poverty on you. You must repent not only for yourself but also for your history. This allows the Courts of Heaven a right to render a cease-and-desist order on your behalf against this spirit of poverty.

The practice of immorality will grant *your poverty* a right to claim you. Proverbs 6:26 tells us that people can be brought to a place of need and poverty when they misbehave sexually.

> *For by means of a harlot*
>
> *A man is reduced to a crust of bread;*
>
> *And an adulteress will prey upon his precious life.*

When people are sexually active outside of marriage the spirit of poverty can claim a right to devour them and their substance. This spirit is a devouring force. Its rights are not just connected to what we do financially. It can claim a right even based on our moral activity. This is why so many people practice other righteous principles of prosperity, yet because of hidden sin in their life the devil has claimed a right to devour them financially.

We cannot practice one principle and think it will nullify another one. We must seek to be holy and pure before the Lord. When we do, the rights of the spirit of poverty are rebuked. The same is true for us concerning immorality as it was for addictions. If there are those in our generational past that were whoremongers and adulterers and given to fornication, the poverty spirit can claim this as a right to deny your prosperity. This must be repented of as well so the poverty spirit has no right to claim its assignment against us. This can be a hidden thing the devil would use to exercise his legal right against us.

Adam and Eve also fell under the control of this spirit of poverty. Remember in Genesis 3:17-19 that God placed a curse on Adam because of his sin and rebellion. A part of this curse was diminished returns from his labor.

> Then to Adam He said, "Because you have heeded the voice of your wife, and have eaten from the tree of which I commanded you, saying, 'You shall not eat of it':
> "Cursed is the ground for your sake;
> In toil you shall eat of it
> All the days of your life.
> Both thorns and thistles it shall bring forth for you,
> And you shall eat the herb of the field.

In the sweat of your face you shall eat bread

Till you return to the ground,

For out of it you were taken;

For dust you are,

And to dust you shall return."

Many falsely believe that work was the curse God placed on Adam. This isn't true. Before the fall of Adam and Eve, Adam was the keeper of the garden. Adam and Eve were to expand the rule of God throughout the whole earth. They were to be busy and enterprising. The curse was not labor. The curse was diminished returns from their labor. The curse was a result of Adam disobeying God and listening to Eve rather than God's voice and command. If we have allowed someone else to have a greater impact and influence in our life than the Lord, this is called idolatry. God and His voice must be first. If we allow another to take that place, a curse of poverty and diminished returns can be the result. We must repent for any and every place we have allowed this. When we do, we undo the legal right the devil would claim. We see this whole issue of diminished returns in Haggai 1:7-9 and its connection to not placing God in the primary position.

Thus says the Lord of hosts: "Consider your ways!
Go up to the mountains and bring wood and build

the temple, that I may take pleasure in it and be glorified," says the Lord. "You looked for much, but indeed it came to little; and when you brought it home, I blew it away. Why?" says the Lord of hosts. "Because of My house that is in ruins, while every one of you runs to his own house."

Notice God says to them, "You looked for much, but indeed it came to little." In other words, there were diminished returns. There was an expectation for so much more than what actually happened. The cause of it was they were placing their own house ahead of the house of God. It caused diminished returns from their labors. The advice of God was to "Consider your ways." Many times the poverty spirit has a right to us because we are placing our own stuff ahead of God's. Again, this is idolatry at work. We must repent and ask the Lord to forgive us so that we can see every legal right of poverty revoked and we become free to prosper.

Another issue that can allow poverty to claim ownership of us is found in Proverbs 11:24-25. We are told that withholding more than is right can actually bring a spirit of poverty on us and give it the right to claim us.

There is one who scatters, yet increases more;
And there is one who withholds more than is right,

But it leads to poverty.

The generous soul will be made rich,

And he who waters will also be watered himself.

Whatever we have been granted is for two primary things. According to Isaiah 55:10, we are given bread to eat and seed to sow.

For as the rain comes down, and the snow from heaven,

And do not return there,

But water the earth,

And make it bring forth and bud,

That it may give seed to the sower

And bread to the eater.

Our financial abilities are for two reasons. They empower us to sow and they empower us to eat. Eating speaks of our needs and wants being supplied. It speaks of provision to have a house to live in, a car to drive, clothes to wear, and food to eat. A portion of the money and finances we have are for these reasons. They are supplied by God to us for these necessary things. However, a portion of our money is to be *seed for the sower*. We must know how to take the *seed portion* and use it to invest with for future harvest. If we don't do this, sooner or later we will run out of *bread to eat*. Also notice that *seed to the sower* is given before *bread to the eater*. In other words, we must make sowing the priority in our lives. Otherwise there will be a day of want and need with nothing to provide for us. This is at least partially what the scripture means when it says, "*withholds more than is right.*"

Notice we are cautioned that this leads to poverty. It can grant the poverty spirit a right in its assignment to devour us. The critical issue is to discern which portion we have in our care is *bread for the eater* and which portion is to be *seed for the sower*. If we eat what we should be sowing, this is *withholding more than is right*. This means our *sowing* must not be sporadic but strategic. A good, successful farmer doesn't sow 50 acres of seed and expect 500 acres of crops. No! He understands a 500-acre harvest requires the sowing of 500 acres of seed. As much as this principle has come under attack by some, it is biblical. This concept didn't begin with the faith teacher or propagators of the prosperity gospel of our day. This idea originated in the New Testament to some degree with the apostle Paul. Second Corinthians 9:6-7 points out this principle as Paul was instructing concerning financial giving.

> *But this I say: He who sows sparingly will also reap sparingly, and he who sows bountifully will also reap bountifully. So let each one give as he purposes*

in his heart, not grudgingly or of necessity; for God
loves a cheerful giver.

First of all, notice that Paul connects the idea of *sowing* with *giving*. This is critical to understand or we might think Paul is talking of planting a natural garden. However, he is clearly speaking of how we give as New Testament believers. His point is that we must give purposely. I like to say, we must *do something on purpose*. When we give as we have purposed in our hearts, we are doing something on purpose in the spirit realm. We are recognizing the principles of sowing and reaping. We know and believe that our harvest is connected to how much we sow. This is what Paul declared. The return I get is joined to my sowing either sparingly or bountifully. This is why a farmer doesn't plant 50 acres of his seed and think he is going to get 500 acres of crops. He knows that 500 acres of harvest are because 500 acres of seed was placed in the ground. I realize that some ministers wittingly and even unwittingly have used these scriptures to manipulate the people of God. This never should be. However, the scripture is true. I would point out two very important guidelines relative to this. First of all, whatever we do must be done in and from faith. We can't just *practice a principle* or *go through the motions*. Our sowing must be motivated from a real dimension of faith. We are told in Romans 14:23 that whatever isn't done in real faith is sin.

> *But he who doubts is condemned if he eats, because he does not eat from faith; for whatever is not from faith is sin.*

This means that I need real biblical faith in my heart when I give. Faith is a result of revelation. Abraham's faith was a result of the word he had heard from God through revelation. Romans 4:18 says the power to believe in Abraham's life came from what he had heard God say.

> *Who, contrary to hope, in hope believed, so that he became the father of many nations, according to what was spoken, "So shall your descendants be."*

The ability of Abraham to wait on the fulfillment of the promise was because he had heard God say, *"So shall your descendants be."* Anytime Abraham began to waiver in faith, he could call to mind what he had heard. The result would be the reignition of real faith in his heart. When we are determining what is seed to sow and what is bread to eat, we must do so from faith. In other words, where do I have real faith operating in my heart. This is what will allow us to do something on purpose. It will also keep us from being manipulated when I discern—do I have real biblical faith for this or am I just doing something in the flesh?

Allow me to give a couple of examples from my own life. I have both sown and given from real faith, but also I have fallen prey to manipulation. Many times people who end up being manipulated are those who have a great heart to please God. This desire will at times drive them to do something in the flesh rather than from the leading of the Holy Spirit. I remember turning on the television and hearing a teacher talk about giving a $1,000 seed. We were in desperate places of need in our life and needed breakthrough. As I listened, I didn't want to miss out on an opportunity to give, obey God, and get our needed breakthrough. I do know that there can be real victories released through these kinds of things. As a result of our current circumstances, my desperation, and the word I was hearing, I made a commitment to give the $1,000. I went to the phone and, if I remember correctly, gave the money on a credit card. As soon as I did it, I regretted it. I had not moved out of faith but rather out of a mixture and a moment of manipulation, whether it was intended or not. As far as I could tell, I never saw anything happen that I could attribute to this momentary activity.

Let me say that I don't *blame* the one who was teaching these ideas. I would even say that I believe in the concepts that were being espoused. It just didn't birth faith in me to function from. The result was nothing occurring from what I gave. Contrast this now to other times in my life when I have seen God move. One that comes to mind is when we were in the early stages of planting a church that grew and became very strong and influential. In the early days, however, we were struggling financially. There wasn't enough to take care of the need of the present expression of this church. As I was praying early one morning, I *heard* the Lord tell me to take $1,000 and give it to a certain other ministry. He showed me there was a log jam in the spirit word and this $1,000 would act as a pry bar and dislodge the logs so they would begin to move again.

A log jam is a reference to the lumber industry where they cut trees down, turn them into logs, and float them down a river to the desired destination. There are times when these logs will get tangled up and stop moving smoothly down the flow of the river. They then have to be dislodged from each other so they can move effectively. This is what I saw in the spirit realm regarding this $1,000 gift I was to sow. It would become the pry bar in the spirit to unlock the logs that were jammed up.

I remember getting up from my place of prayer and going straight to the office, making the check out, and taking it to the post office in those days and mailing it. I did this as quickly as possible so my natural mind wouldn't talk me out of it by reminding me this was the last little bit we had in the church's account. I did this in the early morning. By the afternoon people were bringing money into the office for the church. The situation was completely shifted from being in need to having the need met and even more than enough. Something had unlocked in the spirit world as a result of my obedience. The difference between the two stories I have just related was real faith. I gave one $1,000 gift in the flesh as a result of manipulation and need. I gave the other $1,000 out of faith from hearing the word of the Lord in my heart and gaining His strategy.

It is imperative that we give as we purpose in our heart. However, I believe the purposing must flow from a heart of faith produced from revelation and encounters with God in the spirit realm. Lest you think this doesn't happen very often, I would encourage you that it does. I believe that a lifestyle of giving and sowing produces an ongoing harvest. Psalm 126:6 tells us that whoever habitually operates in these principles will doubtless have an abounding harvest.

> *He who continually goes forth weeping,*
> *Bearing seed for sowing,*
> *Shall doubtless come again with rejoicing,*
> *Bringing his sheaves with him.*

Notice the word *continually*. These principles are not something we sporadically operate in but rather strategically. Again, a farmer doesn't plan and plant his fields once in a while. He actually may plant them several times a year for the harvest that is desired. So we too must develop a lifestyle of practicing sowing with abundance for the harvest we desire and need for our lives, families, and assignments. When we do, the Bible is explicit. We will doubtless see our full harvest manifest in our lives.

This brings me to the other guideline that is essential to not withholding more than is right. Luke 6:38 gives us great insight into how to progressively increase from these principles.

> Give, and it will be given to you: good measure, pressed down, shaken together, and running over will be put into your bosom. For with the same measure that you use, it will be measured back to you.

We are told to give. Notice that as we give and practice the principles, we receive *good measure*. As we continue to discern from the *good measure* we have received what is bread to eat and what is seed to sow, we can increase to the next level of *press down*. As we discover from the *press down* level what is bread and what is seed, we progress to the *shaken together* place. As we continue, we move into the *running over* dimension. This is the realm of abundance. In other words, you can secure for yourself a blessed life by paying attention to the promptings of the Lord. These promptings will allow the Lord to bring you into the life you have dreamed of and desire. These terms all describe new realms of living, blessing, and prosperity. However, it is a progressive process that allows us to walk into these realms.

Notice the last statement of this scripture. It declares, *"For with the same measure that you use, it will be measured back to you."* I was asked this question by the Lord. *"Who determines your level of breakthrough? You or the Lord?"* The answer is *we do!* The problem with most people is that we keep measuring out the same level and somehow think something new will happen for us. New levels of blessings, breakthroughs, and life flow from new levels of measurements being measured out. This requires us taking new steps of faith in our sowing as the Lord mandates and leads us.

Mary and I have learned this principle. I remember when we learned about the First Fruits principle years ago. I will talk about this later in more detail. This was an offering that we brought at least once a year. On this particular year, a deep desire came into my heart to bring a $10,000 offering to the Lord. We didn't have $10,000. We told the Lord that if He would bring that money into our hands, we would bring it to Him as a First Fruits offering. God needed us to bring an offering on a level that would allow Him to bless us in the capacity He intended. The money did, in fact, come into our hands. With a deep heart of love and adoration for the Lord, we brought that offering. I can only say that *all Heaven* broke loose over our lives. When we obeyed the leading of the Lord that was shown us by the deep desire we had, the blessings measured back to us were phenomenal. With the measure we use, it will be measured back to us. As we progressively practice this principle, we can move from *good measure* to *pressed down* to *shaken together* all the way to *running over!* We will set in motion things in the unseen realm that allow the breaking of every poverty spirit and our ability to move into a life of prosperity, wealth, and even riches.

> Lord, as I stand before Your Courts, I ask that any rights the poverty spirit would have to claim me would be revoked. I repent for every place I have come into agreement with this wicked spirit of restriction and limits. I ask, Lord, that You would forgive me and annul any and every right this armored spirit and prowler has claimed against me. Lord, please allow Your blood to speak on my behalf and silence these voices against me in the spirit realm. Lord, I set my heart to be diligent and faithful. I do not allow any laziness to cling to me. I also repent for any places of immorality and uncleanness that would be used to bring me to a piece of

bread (Proverbs 6:26). I also repent for any place of idolatry that would allow the devil to bring diminished returns from my labors. I desire, Lord, for my labors to produce abundantly. I set my heart fully on You, Lord, as the One I serve with my whole heart as I forsake all others. I repent also for holding back more than I should. I want to measure out the right measurements for the blessings of God to overtake me and overwhelm me. Thank you so much, Lord, for bringing me into the prosperity, wealth, and riches of the Lord ordained for me. In Jesus' Name, amen.

CHAPTER 6

GOD: SOCIALIST OR CAPITALIST

In this day of competing economic philosophies, sometimes there can be confusion of how God sees things. At times it is possible to have an idea of God that may not be completely consistent with scripture. This can hinder our prosperity if we therefore are not able to agree with God correctly. For instance, in the parable in Luke 19:24-25 where minas are given to servants to trade with to bring increase, the one to whom one was given did nothing. The Master/Lord of the house dealt very severely with this servant. Among other things, he stripped him of what he had.

> And he said to those who stood by, "Take the mina from him, and give it to him who has ten minas." (But they said to him, "Master, he has ten minas.")

Notice that the other servants protested. They couldn't fathom that the Master was going to give the extra mina that he had taken from the unfaithful servant to the one who already had the most. That didn't seem right. Why not distribute it more *fairly*. Give it to one of the others with less. However, they didn't understand what motivated the Master. He was not a *socialist* who believed in everyone sharing the same. His kingdom was not based on one group doing all the work and others getting the benefit from it when they had not shown the same due effort. He believed in rewarding the ones who had showed the most faithfulness, ingenuity, and energy. To their dismay, the Master was a capitalist. His kingdom operated on principles consistent with capitalism. Capitalism is based on a free market system where creativity, ideas explored, and effort are rewarded. As some have called it, God is a *compassionate capitalist*. In other words, His kingdom operates from principles consistent with capitalism but has a compassionate idealism attached to it. It is not a capitalism where the strong squash the weak. Those who apply principles and become wealthy understand they must help the poor, minister to the weak, and empower others to succeed as they have. They practice these principles consistent with the nature of God.

The reason for this chapter is to expose the false narrative among God's people. There are those in the church that think they are *owed* something, which is what social-ism gives birth to. Socialism also saps motivation and a desire to succeed. If after all, I'm going to get what I want and need regardless of how much effort I put out, then why expend the energy? This births a people who have an entitlement mentality. This is not the standard with which God operates. We are only owed what we produce through the gifting, talents, and empowerments we receive from God. If we adopt this false philosophy, we will never prosper.

The reason the Master gave the mina to the one who had ten was because he had shown the greatest ability to reproduce. *God is a good businessman.* He will not trust His stuff to those who are not going to increase it. So the prin-ciple is simply this—if you want God to trust you with His stuff, do something with what you already have. We cannot allow the *little* that we have to give us an excuse to do nothing. This is what the person with only the one mina presumably did. He allowed the small portion in comparison to what others were given to cause him to not value what he had been entrusted with. We can never do this. We are not judged and evaluated on the basis of what someone else does. We are judged and evaluated on the basis of what we do with what God has given us. If we handle what has been given us righteously and effec-tively, God will trust us with more. This is the principle of

God's Word. The issue isn't what we start with. The issue is what we do with it. Jesus spoke to this in Luke 16:10-12. He shows three distinct areas we must be faithful in to be trusted with more.

> *He who is faithful in what is least is faithful also in much; and he who is unjust in what is least is unjust also in much. Therefore if you have not been faithful in the unrighteous mammon, who will commit to your trust the true riches? And if you have not been faithful in what is another man's, who will give you what is your own?*

First, we must be faithful in the least. God is watching. Not just how we handle money, but how we steward everything we have been trusted with. I remember when I moved to Tyler, Texas to begin my training for ministry. The route God took me to prepare me for my life of ministry was under an apostolic father who mentored me into maturity. When Mary and I moved to this location in 1980, we set up our lives in a rented house. When we unloaded the furniture in this house, the yard needed mowing, the hedges were unkept, and things were just shabby. I wasn't concerned at all. I was there to get ready to touch the world for Jesus. I was going to have a large, influential ministry that would impact nations. This was my opinion as I began this journey in my early 20s. The condition of the house I lived in meant nothing to me.

I will never forget as we got things unloaded and the pastor, my apostolic father, was there encouraging me and helping us get settled. He then said this to me. *"Robert, I do not want to see you at the church until this yard is mowed and these hedges are trimmed."* I was flabbergasted. Didn't he know who I was meant to be? What difference did the condition of this house have to do with anything? I was there to change the world. What I came to understand was he was requiring faithfulness in the *little things* of me. He knew what I didn't yet know. Faithfulness had to be born in me in all things. If I learned to be faithful in what didn't seem to matter, God would trust me with much more. However, if I wasn't faithful in the least, I couldn't and wouldn't be trusted with the big things.

It's like the scene in the *Karate Kid* when Daniel is being trained by Mr. Miyagi. Daniel wants to learn karate. Instead, Mr. Miyagi has him polishing his cars and doing other chores. Daniel becomes very frustrated and almost quits. He doesn't realize that through these menial tasks and jobs he has been doing, he is learning movements and methods that were required for his karate skills. To his amazement, when Mr. Miyagi begins his *real lessons* in karate, Daniel has already mastered moves that came from the menial tasks he had been doing. His faithfulness in small things had produced in him what he would need to be a champion. So it is with us. If we can learn faithfulness in what doesn't seem to matter, God will entrust to us what does matter. The lessons and formation of our character from being faithful in the small things will be what we use in the big things. This is what happened to David. Psalm 78:70-72 gives us insight into how God trained David to be king.

> *He also chose David His servant,*
>
> *And took him from the sheepfolds;*
>
> *From following the ewes that had young He brought him,*
>
> *To shepherd Jacob His people,*
>
> *And Israel His inheritance.*
>
> *So he shepherded them according to the integrity of his heart,*
>
> *And guided them by the skillfulness of his hands.*

Very clearly God chose David after he learned lessons from being a shepherd boy among his father's sheep. The faithfulness he learned in that place prepared him to shepherd the inheritance of God—His people. God was able to trust David with this huge responsibility because of his faithfulness in the hidden place of the sheepfold. In these places where no one but God saw him, the Lord developed the right heart in David and the set of skills necessary to the task everyone would see and applaud. The question is, will we be found faithful in the small, hidden task committed to us by God? If we can be, then the larger places of purpose and destiny will be ours!

A second place we are tested in and must be found faithful is in the *unrighteous mammon*. This is speaking of money and material things. Jesus is clear that God uses these areas to test us and prove us. When we are found faithful in these then we will be trusted with the *true riches*. The true riches are the favor of God, anointing, authority in the spirit world, influence, wisdom, and other intangibles. God is looking for those He can trust with these places. However, the testing ground is how we handle money. This involves paying our bills on time, budgeting our income, and our giving practices. If we steward money well, then not only will God trust us with more, but it will allow Him to trust us with what money can't buy. Many people would contend that if they had more money *then* they could be faithful. My experience has been that God wants to see if we can be faithful even when there isn't enough. If we had an endless stream of finances in these periods of our lives, then there would really be no test. In other words, the test is—what will I do with my money when it is hard to make it work? Will I obey the principles of the Lord when it costs me something?

I remember when Mary and I were training for ministry in the early days. We lived in a 14-foot by 80-foot mobile home. We had four children. Our finances were very tight. There never seemed to be enough to go around. The money always ran out before the month did. We were faithful tithers and givers in the church. We always took 10 percent of our income off the gross of our pay and honored the Lord with it. In the natural this seemed ludicrous. There was actually a time when we gave our tithe and couldn't pay some of our other bills. I remember this particular month when our electricity was turned off as well as our gas. Not only was this humiliating but very stressful. My parents happened to be at our house at this time. I was mortified. In response to what was happening, my mother said to me, "*It looks like y'all should pack it up and come home.*" She was frustrated for us and her grandkids over how we were living. We weren't happy either. However, I knew we were doing what we were supposed to be doing.

I said to her with great respect, "*Didn't you and Daddy go through hard places at our age?*" She responded that they had. I then said to her, "*Then why would you cheat us out of this for our destiny and future?*" I wasn't really being wise; I was just trying to justify what was happening. My mother being who she was, when she saw that I was set, she relented and agreed. I was amazed at what came out of my mouth in that moment. It was a hard and difficult place, but we stayed faithful with our money to the Lord and as much as we possibly could with our bills being paid on time. We did live under much stress during those days. Yet we endeavored with all manner of effort to be true. What I discovered is that none of this goes unnoticed by the Lord. It is recorded and known in Heaven. I believe much of the blessing that Mary and I live under today is because of our decisions in those days to be faithful. We sought with every part of our beings to be faithful with the unrighteous mammon. This has purchased for us a place of great favor and blessing before God.

The third and final area that we must be true in is with what belongs to others. We are told that if we aren't faithful in what belongs to others, then God will not give us our own. Wherever you are serving, working, or ministering, be faithful with what God has given to another person. God is watching how we serve others and what he has entrusted to them. If we are judged and found faithful in this, we are setting our future for God to give us our own. I served my pastor and apostolic father for eight years. I never undermined him. I never thought he owed me something. I never expected anything. I did to the absolute best of my ability what I was asked to do. I cleaned to church as the janitor. I mowed the grass. I was at every service three to four times on a normal week. My family and I were fixtures in this house. We served with excitement and great desire. God saw this and rewarded me with my own. The ministry I have today is because God counted me faithful putting me into the ministry. First Timothy 1:12 says this of Paul:

> And I thank Christ Jesus our Lord who has enabled me, because He counted me faithful, putting me into the ministry.

Notice that the enablement came out of God counting Paul faithful. So often we think gifting or abilities are something we just have or develop. However, Paul understood that his strength and power in ministry was given to him because God had judged him faithful. I was never the most gifted person in the situation. Whether it was athletics, academia, preaching, and even social interaction. So often I have felt awkward and untrained. By nature this would have caused me to draw away into obscurity and the shadows. I knew though that this would work against what I was actually made for. I therefore fought against these tendencies and tried. To my amazement I would discover anointing and empowerments I didn't know I had. Even in this I still had a sense of not measuring up. Even my own pastor said of me, *"I didn't know if this boy was going to make it or not."* He didn't mean this as being critical. He was actually boasting in the grace that

God extended to me that allowed me to succeed. Everyone could see I wasn't highly gifted. No one questioned my heart, but they were not convinced of my ability. So how did I make it? How did I do it? I sought to stay faithful and believe that my God would bless what I did have but would also reward me with what I didn't have. This is exactly what He has done. He has enabled me. This enablement has come from being faithful. God rewards those who diligently seek Him (see Hebrews 11:6). Whatever ability I have has come from the grace of God in my life and not my own production.

The other thing Paul said was that as a result of his faithfulness God *put* him in the ministry. He didn't maneuver or manipulate his way into a position. God *put* him there. I have always been a busy person. However, at this stage of my life I am busier than I have ever been. I lead a global ministry, I travel extensively, I lead a global house of prayer with leaders all over the world, I am an author writing many books a year, I have my own weekly television show, I host several conferences a year, I am the apostolic leader that many churches/ministries connect with, and even have other responsibilities. As I said, I am busy. There are times that people look at my life and question my *busyness.* They go so far as to, at least imply, that I am being irresponsible by doing as much as I do at this stage in my life.

One day I was meditating on this and thought, "*Maybe they're right.*" Immediately I felt God speak this scripture in First Timothy 1:12 to me. I felt He said, "*Your busyness isn't your doing. It is a result of Me putting you in the ministry. My hand and favor being on you is what is producing this. I have need of you. Just be faithful.*" This settled it for me. This is not to say I shouldn't be wise and discerning as I work and operate and plan my schedule. However, I felt God wanted me to know I wasn't producing this; He was. This all stemmed from my faithfulness to what was another man's. My admonishment to anyone who wants to sow seeds for their success and prosperity is—find another to serve. If we will do this, God will reward us with our own. If you want to be a successful businessman, find a businessman to serve. If you want to be in government, find someone in that realm to serve. If you want to be in ministry, find a ministry to serve and connect. This is the simple yet powerful principle that will speak on your behalf for decades to come as you seek to prosper and increase in the realms granted you by God.

> Lord, as I stand in Your Courts, I repent for any wrong idea and concept I have had about You. I ask for perpetual revelation of You to enlighten my heart and mind concerning You and Your ways. As I come to a new awareness of You, I ask that I might more effectively agree with You

and petition You in Your Courts. Lord, I repent for anything in me that would think I am owed something or that I am entitled to something. I realize, Lord, that You are looking for faithfulness. I ask that by Your grace this would be birthed in me that You might trust me with Your riches. Lord, I ask that I might steward them into increase for You and Your kingdom. Lord, empower me, I ask, to be faithful and diligent with that which is Yours. In Jesus' Name, amen.

CHAPTER 7

LEGALISM OR GRACE

One of the most significant adjustments God made in my life was to move me out of serving Him in legalism and into serving Him in grace. Let me explain it to you the way it happened. As the husband and father in our family, I have always carried a sense of responsibility to see that needs were met and even wants and desires fulfilled. With the size family we had—Mary, me, and six children—this was no small task. Not only did I work diligently and try to plan methodically, I prayed.

When I say I prayed, I mean I prayed hard. I still do. I knew then and do now that there was no way I could in my own strength provide for my family the way I wanted them to be provided for. So in addition to work and giving, I prayed—diligently. As one who was called by God into vocational ministry, I never wanted my children to think they were denied something because their father was a preacher. I detest this. I have watched children of ministers grow to be bitter and angry adults because they did without. Perhaps they didn't do without what they needed, but definitely what they wanted. I did not want this to be my children's experience. I wanted my children's experience to be just the opposite. I wanted them to think they had privileges others didn't have because of the ministry.

I think we succeeded on some level. Of our six children, five of them work full time in the ministry and are successful at what they do. I tell Mary that in the midst of the hard places we walked, obviously our children came away with a *good taste* in their mouth about ministry. Ultimately, they are in ministry because of the call of God. However, they didn't struggle with it because they lived a blessed life growing up in a minister's home. This experience was because I did what I was called to do but also because I made it my practice to petition the Lord for His blessings and increase into our lives. As I would do this on a daily basis, I would go through the *list* of things I needed to see provision for. I would ask the Lord for our house to be provided for, cars provided, children's school tuition, children's cars (as they got older), and the normal needs/wants of a family. I would religiously go through this routine every day, reminding God of what I needed Him to provide. The amazing thing was God always met everything I petitioned Him for. Exactly what I asked for would be provided and come into our family. One day when I was in prayer and about to go through this routine again, I heard the Lord say to me, *"Stop agreeing with Me."* In one sense I was caught off guard. On the other hand, I immediately knew what the Lord was referring to. Matthew 20:1-16 tells the parable of a man hiring laborers for his vineyard. He goes out several times throughout the day and hires different groups to work in the vineyard. He begins at the start of the day in Matthew 20:1-2.

> *For the kingdom of heaven is like a landowner who went out early in the morning to hire laborers for his vineyard. Now when he had agreed with the laborers for a denarius a day, he sent them into his vineyard.*

When the Lord said, *"Stop agreeing with Me,"* this is the scripture that came immediately to mind. I knew I was about to receive a revelation from the Lord. When we read the entire parable, we find that this first group *agreed* with the landowner. This means in essence they had a contract with him. All the other groups didn't do this. When hired, they went on an entirely different basis of *whatever is right.* Matthew 20:3-4 shows these groups after the first group responding to the landowner.

> *And he went out about the third hour and saw others standing idle in the marketplace, and said to them,*

"You also go into the vineyard, and whatever is right
I will give you." So they went.

Who takes a job and doesn't ask what they are going
to be paid before they begin work? Not anyone I know.
Anytime I took a job, I always knew what I was going
to make before I gave out the effort. However, these said
they would work on the basis of *whatever is right*. In other
words, they trusted the generosity, liberality, goodness,
and kindness of the landowner. These groups and the
basis on which they served speak of serving under the
law and serving under grace. The first group were the
Jews Jesus was sent to first. Their *agreement or contract* was
Moses' law. This law basically said what their responsibilities were and what God would do as they met them. This
was the agreement. The other groups, however, were the
Gentiles who came in after the Jews rejected Jesus as the
Messiah. They did not come in operating under the law
but under grace. They had a confidence in the goodness,
kindness, generosity, and liberality of the landowner, who
is the Lord, while the vineyard is His kingdom. When the
Lord said to me, *"Stop agreeing with Me,"* I knew He was
admonishing me to stop being ritualistic and legalistic in
my request of Him for my provision. I immediately that
day changed the way I petitioned the Lord concerning my
needs and wants. I began like this:

Lord, as I come before Your Courts and Counsel, I do not agree with You. I repent for approaching You as one under the law. I say before You that I live under Your graciousness. I serve You, Lord, as the owner of the vineyard, Your kingdom. I thank You that from Your goodness, kindness, liberality, and generosity as the owner of the vineyard You provide for me. I serve You on the basis of whatever is right. I trust Your graciousness into my life.

I began to pray a prayer like this as I requested from the Lord His provisions into my life. *Immediately* things began to change. Exponential increase started coming into my life. Instead of needs and desires just being met, multiplication occurred and there was much more than enough. We began to witness the blessings and bounty of the Lord on a whole new level. The only thing different I was doing was praying out of His grace and not being a legalist in my heart and mind. I then began to see deeper revelation from Matthew 20. I saw that those who agreed were taken care of, but only in what they had agreed for. The other groups, however, experienced great and even unexpected blessings from the owner of the vineyard. Let me list a few things that happened for them. First of all, even though they were hired last they were paid first. This was what Jesus said, *"The last shall be first and the first last"* (Matthew

20:16). This means that when we move from legalism to grace in our lives we allow God to promote us. Those who seem to be forgotten, left out, abused, and even ridiculed are set in places of prosperity and influence. The second thing that I would mention is the one who worked one hour was given 12 hours' worth of wages. Matthew 20:9 says they actually received the normal wage for a 12-hour workday which was a denarius.

> *And when those came who were hired about the elev-*
> *enth hour, they each received a denarius.*

This means that if someone was paid $10 per hour, the twelve-hour workday, which was common in this culture, would mean they received $120 for their full day's work. The goodness of the owner, however, paid the one who worked only an hour the full day's wage. If this rate was multiplied out for a yearly income and they worked six days a week for 52 weeks in a year at the rate of $120 per hour, the income would be $449,280 per year. *Wow!* This gives us some kind of an idea of the extravagance with which this owner was blessing the workers who trusted His goodness. On the other hand, the ones who agreed at the rate they were paid would only make $37,440. This is simply designed to show us the difference between what happens when we serve God from grace rather than legalism and ritual. We free the Lord to manifest His goodness toward us. The third thing that can happen when we serve from grace is we free the Lord's passion to be stirred toward us. Matthew 20:14 declares that the owner wished to bless these who trusted His kindness and left their wage to him.

> *Take what is yours and go your way. I wish to give to this last man the same as to you.*

Anytime we place our faith and confidence in the goodness of God, He will not fail us. In fact, our faith in who He is seems to move His heart and passion toward us. When we step out of ritualistic service to Him because we subtly think our efforts impress Him and move into serving Him from a love relationship, great things can occur. After I began to operate in this principle, I went to a church that had less than 100 people in attendance. I ministered as I always did on the Court of Heaven. I simply spoke the principles God had given me. I always go on the *basis of whatever is right* in these settings. I do not *agree*. In other words, I don't require a certain amount to go and minister. To my amazement, in this small setting over $20,000 came into the ministry. There is no way in the natural that this should have happened. I knew the Lord was manifesting His passion toward me because I was serving Him on the basis of whatever is right. If we can shift and put our confidence in the Lord and who He is revealed to be through the grace of Jesus Christ, exponential increase can occur. A fourth thing that happened as we served from His grace was God would use us to adjust others' perspectives about Him. Matthew 20:15 shows the owner declaring to those who complained that He can do what He wants with His own stuff. He then makes an astounding statement.

> *Is it not lawful for me to do what I wish with my own things? Or is your eye evil because I am good?*

People who are bound in religion and ritualistic service to God tend to have a problem with how good God really is. The first group griped and complained about how much the other groups were being paid. This is because they didn't have a revelation of the goodness, generosity, liberality, and kindness of the landowner. Therefore, they were filled with judgment, criticism, accusations, and even condemnation. However, the owner was using his generosity toward these to unveil the wickedness in the hearts of the first group. He was seeking to move them to jealousy as they began to see who the landowner really was.

The Lord is looking for those He can bless so abundantly that it will manifest who He is to others. Those who get blessed this way may encounter persecution and ridicule. The result though will be not only us coming into new dimensions of wealth and increase, but others beginning to see God in a different light and understanding. My cry to God is, *"Here I am Lord, use me."* My cry is that the Lord would bless me beyond what my effort can produce. Those who were paid these exuberant wages could not produce this themselves. This was the goodness of God at work. My efforts can never do what the goodness of God will do in my life. I therefore pray for this to occur so that God's kindness might be manifested in me, to me, and through me. I ask that He would show forth His glory and receive honor and praise through His blessing of my life, family, and ministry. To Him belongs the honor and glory!

> Lord, as I stand in Your Courts, I petition You.
> I ask, Lord, that I would move from any place
> of legalism I am serving from into Your grace.
> I ask that You might bring a revelation of this
> into my heart. As I stand in this place, Lord,
> I declare I do not agree with You. I say I serve
> You on the basis of whatever is right. I ask as I
> do this that promotion would come. I ask that
> Your passion would be stirred toward me for
> wealth and prosperity. I ask that exponential
> increase would come to my life. I ask, Lord,
> that You would do in me and through me what
> my labors could never produce. Use me, Lord,
> as an example of Your kindness through Your
> increase in my life. Let others' perspectives of

You change because of how much You bless me. Lord, I declare I trust Your goodness, kindness, liberality, and generosity as the owner of the vineyard. Thank You so much for loving me. In Jesus' Name, amen.

CHAPTER 8

MONEY TALKS

We've probably all heard the phrase "*money talks*." It's the idea that whoever has money has influence. This is absolutely true. However, we might be amazed to know that money actually does have a *voice* in the spirit world. Money gives testimony and judicial witness either for us or against us in the realms of the unseen dimension. This is why whatever we do with our money in the natural world, its influence is felt far beyond what we see in the seen realm. Hebrews 7:8 gives us some intriguing insight into this idea.

> *Here mortal men receive tithes, but there he receives them, of whom it is witnessed that he lives.*

The overview of this scripture is that Jesus is our High Priest after the Order of Melchizedek. We are no longer under the Levitical priesthood but now have a High Priest who lives forever. When the Bible speaks of *mortal men*, it is speaking of the Levitical priesthood that has passed away. It has been replaced with a new and better priesthood ministering on our behalf. It is the Melchizedek Order where Jesus is the High Priest. We are told that when we bring our tithes, Jesus as the High Priest of this order *receives them*. This means that all the erroneous teaching that we shouldn't tithe because we aren't any longer under the law is *wrong!* We do not tithe under the law, but we do tithe in honor of who Jesus is as our High Priest in and from the Melchizedek Order. In fact, my tithe makes a declaration in the spirit world that *He lives!*

Every time I bring my tithe to the Lord, which is 10 percent of my income, I am making a statement in the spirit world. My statement that is recorded in Heaven is that "*I believe He lives.*" This statement is a very powerful and strong witness of my hope, faith, and confidence in Jesus' work for me and on my behalf. The word *witnessed* in the scripture is the Greek word *martureo*. It means to "testify, give evidence, and bear record." Wow! When I bring my tithe to the Lord in honor of who He is and what He has done for me, I am giving testimony in the heavenly realm that I believe He lives! My money is speaking and establishing things on my behalf in the Courts of Heaven. My tithe causes it to be recorded in Heaven of my total and only hope being in Jesus and who He is for me.

I was in Germany doing a conference. In the conference I felt led to speak concerning these things. I begin to declare through the translator, "*What brain-dead, idiotic, stupid, unlearned person would take one tenth of their income and give it to a ministry or church?*" As I spoke this, all the Germans were looking at me as a crass and insulting American. They must have been wondering what I was going to do or say next. As I had their attention, I then proclaimed, "*Only those who believe He lives.*" Tithing is a declaration that I believe He lives. He is not dead in the grave. They didn't steal His body away and contrive the greatest hoax of history. We haven't followed skillfully crafted fantasies. Jesus is in fact alive. He is at the right hand of the Father interceding as my High Priest after the Order of Melchizedek. When I bring my tithe in the natural, He receives it there in the spiritual as a testimony of my faith and belief!

My testimony of my tithe and money also does something else very powerfully. It connects me to the present-day life that Jesus is living for my benefit. When I declare through my tithe that *He lives,* it isn't just a confession I am giving. This confession makes a connection. It allows what Jesus is doing as my High Priest to have impact in my life and situations. Hebrews 7:25 tells us that Jesus is interceding for us from His heavenly dimension.

Therefore He is also able to save to the uttermost those who come to God through Him, since He always lives to make intercession for them.

Notice that the purpose of His present life is to intercede. When I confess through my tithe of my belief that He is alive, I am also connecting to that life. The life that Jesus is living is a life of intercession for me. My testimony through my tithe causes me to gain benefit from the prayer life of Jesus! In other words, my tithe connects me to the present-day ministry of intercession that Jesus is functioning in. I get the full benefit of what He is doing for me because of the testimony of my tithe connecting me to it. I get saved and born again because of His death, burial, and resurrection. However, I get saved to the uttermost, or the fullness of what He died for me to have, through His present intercession for me. Jesus is praying me into the fullness of His work on my behalf. Salvation isn't just about going to Heaven after I die. Salvation is about that which God has for me now as well. We have a covenant with God through the body and blood of Jesus that promises life, healing, health, prosperity, wealth, harmony in family, and any other thing necessary for life and godliness. Through the intercession of Jesus, we are prayed into the reality of this. My tithe connects me to this intercession that is a result of the life Jesus presently is living. So my tithe has great ramifications in the spirit world. The testimony it is releasing is creating a connection to Jesus' prayer life for me! Again, wow!

The prayer life of Jesus for us is very significant. When Jesus came to the tomb of Lazarus, Martha made a powerful statement in John 11:22.

> *But even now I know that whatever You ask of God,*
> *God will give You.*

Whatever Jesus asks of the Father, the Father will give it to Him. This is the power of Jesus' prayer to the Father. The Father never denies Jesus what He is asking. If Jesus asks for us, the Father will grant it and give it. So if I can be rightly connected to the prayer life of Jesus for me through my tithe, I can get the benefit of Jesus' intercession for me toward the Father. In other words, sometimes my confidence shouldn't be in my prayer life but in the prayer life of Jesus for me. When I am connected to it through my tithe, amazing answers can come.

A couple of testimonies emphasize this great truth. My son contacted me one day and asked if I would be willing to get on a three-way call with someone who was diagnosed with stage-4 cancer. I agreed to do so. As I engaged this person, I asked if there was any cancer in their generational history. They informed me that their grandmother and mother had both died from cancer. I told them this was because the devil had claimed a legal right against the family line. The devil was claiming the right to kill them with cancer just as he had done their mother and grandmother. This would be a result from some iniquity in the bloodline and/or a covenant made with demonic powers in their ancestry either purposely or without intent. I informed them that they needed to repent for this and take ownership of it. They must ask for the blood of Jesus to speak on their behalf and annul the legal right Satan was using to afflict them with cancer and then death. Even if they had no awareness of what was being used to make such a claim, by faith they could set in place the judicial verdict of the cross on their behalf. Colossians 2:14 is part of the stated verdict of the cross.

Having wiped out the handwriting of requirements that was against us, which was contrary to us. And He has taken it out of the way, having nailed it to the cross.

The handwriting of requirements spoken of are the cases Satan presents against us that allow him to claim the right to kill, steal, and destroy. When we in faith agree with and set in place what Jesus did on the cross, we legally can see the claims of Satan annulled and revoked. I led this person in this type of prayer. It went something like this:

Lord, as I come before Your Courts, I repent for my sins, transgressions, and iniquities. I ask for Your blood, Jesus, to speak on my behalf and annul every voice of Satan demanding the right to devour me based on my unrighteous activity. Lord, I would remind this Court, the Court of Heaven, that when Jesus died on the cross every handwriting of requirement against me was taken out of the way. It was nailed to the cross with Jesus. Therefore, whatever Satan is using against me died with Jesus. I ask that this would be set in place and every sin and transgression, plus every iniquity or covenant with demons, would now be annulled and revoked. I ask that their right to speak against me is now silenced. I ask that the rights being claimed to devour me with this cancer is now abolished in Jesus' Name. Amen.

As I led this person in this prayer, I then sensed the Holy Spirit nudging me to lead this one in a prayer I had never prayed before nor led anyone in. I asked them to pray after me in this manner:

Lord, as I stand before Your Courts, I would remind this Court that I am a tither. Lord, it is the joy of my heart to honor You as my High

Priest with my tithe. With my tithe I proclaim that You live. I also connect to Your life on my behalf with my tithe. I join myself to You as my High Priest and Intercessor. I ask, Lord, that You would now pray on my behalf before the Father. I know, Lord, that whatever You asked the Father He will do. I join myself to Your life and intercession and ask that Your prayer for me would now cause healing to flow into my body and this cancer would be destroyed and removed. In Jesus' Name, amen.

As we prayed, I sensed a moving of God's presence. We hung up greatly encouraged. Within a few days we began to get notice that the tumors the cancer had caused on the body were shrinking away. This person's health began to be restored. Instead of a death sentence, God gave them back their life. It was because we approached the Courts with the blood, annulled the devil's right he was claiming, but also approached God on the status the person's tithe gave them. As we did, the benefits that are ours from the cross were implemented and released to this one. There is great power in connecting to Jesus' life through what our tithe is testifying before His Courts.

Another testimony I heard was about a situation in a third-world country where an American evangelist was ministering. It was in a desert area where a lot of indigent people lived. As these meetings would be held, salvations, healings, and deliverances would occur and people would be baptized to declare they were walking with Jesus now. As a result of the dryness and lack of water in these places, a hole or pit would be dug in the desert, lined with plastic, and filled with water. This became the baptismal. During one of the morning sessions, the two-year-old son of the host leader slipped away from the one who was responsible for caring for him. He fell into this water-filled hole and drowned. It was a while before they found him and his body had already begun to bloat as it lay in this pool. When he was found they ran and interrupted the morning session. They informed the host leader what had happened to his son. This leader ran and took his drowned son and ran into a shack that was on the property. All the people gathered around this shack and began to peer into the shack through the cracks in the wall. The leader was sitting on the bed, rocking back and forth, cradling the body of his dead son. He was crying out in Spanish.

The American evangelist was one of those looking through the cracks in the wall of the shack. As he gazed at this heart-breaking spectacle, he asked one standing by what the leader was saying as he cried to God. They told him he was saying, "*But God, I'm a tither. But God, I'm a tither.*" As this man cried out, all of a sudden the glory of God came into that shack. The dead, drowned boy began to cough and sputter and was resuscitated. His body began to shrink back to normal. He was completely healed and raised from the dead. What an awesome God we serve. Hallelujah! This miracle occurred because this leader connected to the present life of Jesus through his tithe. His tithe was speaking and testifying in the Courts of Heaven that he believed He lived. Because of this, the present-day life of Jesus entered that shack and brought life to a dead, drowned boy! It was the testimony of this man's tithe that allowed this sign and wonder to occur. Our tithe is speaking in the Courts of Heaven for us. It is declaring we believe and connect to Jesus' present-day life and activity for us.

Our money talks. It doesn't matter whether we want it to or not. Our money is either speaking for us or it can be speaking against us. We have seen how it can speak for us as it testifies of what we believe. However, money used improperly and with a wrong attitude can actually speak against us. James 5:3-4 shows us money releasing a testimony we don't want it to.

> *Your gold and silver are corroded, and their corro-*
> *sion will be a witness against you and will eat your*
> *flesh like fire. You have heaped up treasure in the last*
> *days. Indeed the wages of the laborers who mowed*

> *your fields, which you kept back by fraud, cry out;*
> *and the cries of the reapers have reached the ears of*
> *the Lord of Sabaoth.*

Notice the word *witness* that is used. This is the Greek word *marturion*. It means "evidence given, a testimony." Their wealth and its corrosion would speak and give evidence against them. It actually goes further though and declares that the *wages held back are crying out*. Notice, not the laborers but the wages that were rightfully theirs that the rich were holding back and not releasing to them— they were crying out. This is because money has a voice and does talk. We see from this principle that when money is *held back* it begins to testify against the ones *keeping it back*. This can be businesspeople who don't give what was agreed on to workers. This can be God's people who don't give what God has commanded. This can be people who promise things to God and don't fulfill them. Anytime money is held back, it can speak against us. Its testimony can be used by the devil to build a case against us and deny us our breakthrough and prosperity. This is why we are told not to promise something and then renege on the promises. Ecclesiastes 5:4-6 gives us advice concerning holding things back.

> *When you make a vow to God, do not delay to pay it;*
> *For He has no pleasure in fools.*

Pay what you have vowed—

Better not to vow than to vow and not pay.

Do not let your mouth cause your flesh to sin, nor say before the messenger of God that it was an error. Why should God be angry at your excuse and destroy the work of your hands?

The devil takes occasion from the Word of God to demand the right to devour us when we violate God's Word. We are told that if we promise something and don't fulfill it, the works of our hands can be destroyed. This is because something has been held back that was to be given. The money held back begins to speak against us and the devil demands the right to devour. To really understand this, we must recognize God's view of the *devoted thing*. The *devoted thing* is that which God demands and/or we promise of our own free will to give. In other words, it is devoted to the Lord. In Numbers 18:14 while speaking to the priest, God declares that which is *devoted* to be given to them as a portion of their livelihood.

Every devoted thing in Israel shall be yours.

The word *devoted* is the Hebrew word *cherem*. It means "a doomed object or that which is designated to be destroyed." In other words, the Lord is declaring that when something is dedicated or devoted to the Lord, in our minds it must be doomed and destroyed. We give it so completely that we no longer have a claim on it in any form. It is as if it is destroyed and no longer exists for us. This word *cherem* was used of the city of Jericho in Joshua 6:17-19 when God told them they could not take or touch anything in the city. All had to be destroyed and/or brought into the Lord's treasury.

> Now the city shall be doomed by the Lord to destruction, it and all who are in it. Only Rahab the harlot shall live, she and all who are with her in the house, because she hid the messengers that we sent. And you, by all means abstain from the accursed things, lest you become accursed when you take of the accursed things, and make the camp of Israel a curse, and trouble it. But all the silver and gold, and vessels of bronze and iron, are consecrated to the Lord; they shall come into the treasury of the Lord.

The words *doomed* and *accursed* are the Hebrew word *cherem*. Jericho was the first city of conquest. God claimed it for Himself. He always claims the first. He is to be honored with the first always. He cautioned them not to touch the accursed thing. In other words, if they laid hold of what God claimed for Himself it would cause a curse to come on them. This is exactly what happened when Achan took silver, gold, and a Babylonian garment. In his mind I'm sure he thought it couldn't hurt. However, it was an accursed thing because it had been *devoted* to the Lord. The result was the blessing of God lifting off the nation and army of Israel and them being defeated in battle. Joshua 7:1-12 is a lengthy verse of scripture. However, it shows Achan's sin and therefore the curse coming on the whole nation of Israel and allowing their enemies to defeat them.

> *But the children of Israel committed a trespass regarding the accursed things, for Achan the son of Carmi, the son of Zabdi, the son of Zerah, of the tribe of Judah, took of the accursed things; so the anger of the Lord burned against the children of Israel.*
>
> *Now Joshua sent men from Jericho to Ai, which is beside Beth Aven, on the east side of Bethel, and spoke to them, saying, "Go up and spy out the country." So the men went up and spied out Ai. And they returned to Joshua and said to him, "Do not let all the people go up, but let about two or three thousand men go up and attack Ai. Do not weary all the people there, for the people of Ai are few." So about three thousand men went up there from the people, but they fled before the men of Ai. And the men of Ai struck down about thirty-six men, for they chased them from before the gate as far as Shebarim, and*

struck them down on the descent; therefore the hearts of the people melted and became like water.

Then Joshua tore his clothes, and fell to the earth on his face before the ark of the Lord until evening, he and the elders of Israel; and they put dust on their heads. And Joshua said, "Alas, Lord God, why have You brought this people over the Jordan at all—to deliver us into the hand of the Amorites, to destroy us? Oh, that we had been content, and dwelt on the other side of the Jordan! O Lord, what shall I say when Israel turns its back before its enemies? For the Canaanites and all the inhabitants of the land will hear it, and surround us, and cut off our name from the earth. Then what will You do for Your great name?"

So the Lord said to Joshua: "Get up! Why do you lie thus on your face? Israel has sinned, and they have also transgressed My covenant which I commanded them. For they have even taken some of the accursed things, and have both stolen and deceived; and they have also put it among their own stuff. Therefore the children of Israel could not stand before their enemies, but turned their backs before their enemies, because they have become doomed to destruction. Neither will I be with you anymore, unless you destroy the accursed from among you."

When Joshua begins to complain to God that He isn't being faithful to His word, the Lord tells him to *"get up!"* The Lord lets him know the reason for this defeat was they had *touched the devoted thing.* This allowed the enemy the legal right to defeat them. That which should have been speaking for them began to speak against them because it was *held back.* The result was Joshua had to search things out and discover who and what had been done. When this happened, the blessing of God was reinstated on the nation and the army of Israel. They marched through the rest of the land and took it without defeat or consequence.

The whole issue was their unrighteous handling of the *devoted thing.* When a devoted thing is withheld or touched, it grants the devil the legal right to consume. Our money and finances either speak for us or against us. The issue is how we are handling what belongs to God either by His word or our free will. We must make sure that our money is releasing the right sound on our behalf. A large part of this is connected to that which is devoted to the Lord. For instance, it would appear this was the problem concerning Ananias and Sapphira in Acts 5:1-11. The scripture says they committed to bring all they had gained through selling property but then reneged on it.

But a certain man named Ananias, with Sapphira his wife, sold a possession. And he kept back part of the proceeds, his wife also being aware of it, and brought a certain part and laid it at the apostles' feet. But Peter said, "Ananias, why has Satan filled your heart to lie to the Holy Spirit and keep back part of the price of the land for yourself? While it remained, was it not your own? And after it was sold, was it not in your own control? Why have you conceived this thing in your heart? You have not lied to men but to God."

Then Ananias, hearing these words, fell down and breathed his last. So great fear came upon all those who heard these things. And the young men arose and wrapped him up, carried him out, and buried him.

Now it was about three hours later when his wife came in, not knowing what had happened. And Peter answered her, "Tell me whether you sold the land for so much?"

She said, "Yes, for so much."

Then Peter said to her, "How is it that you have agreed together to test the Spirit of the Lord? Look, the feet of those who have buried your husband are at the door, and they will carry you out." Then immediately she fell down at his feet and breathed her last. And the young men came in and found her dead, and carrying her out, buried her by her husband. So great *fear came upon all the church and upon all who heard these things.*

Peter said they had lied to the Holy Spirit. In other words, they promised a certain amount but didn't fulfill it. They didn't lie to men but to God. When they claimed to have brought all of it but kept back part of it, they touched the *devoted thing.* The whole of it became a devoted thing when they with their mouth said they were giving all. The result was judgment being pronounced against them. They both died because of this infraction against God. Judgment was enacted because they violated the principle of the devoted thing. This became a legal right for judgment to be executed against them. There was testimony in Heaven against them from the money they *held back.*

Could it be that Satan took the words of their mouth and accused them before God? Their activity left God no place of redemption for them in this situation. Based on their violation of the word of God, Satan demanded judgment on them. Remember, money held back from what it is designated for can speak against us. I believe this is what happened to Ananias and Sapphira. Peter's declaration of judgment was based on the testimony of their held-back money before the Courts. We must make sure we are handling our money correctly so that the testimony it is giving is for us and not against us.

The centurion Cornelius in Acts 10:1-4 had an encounter with an angel sent to him. The reason the angel came was because Heaven had been impacted with his prayers and giving.

> *There was a certain man in Caesarea called Cornelius, a centurion of what was called the Italian Regiment, a devout man and one who feared God with all his household, who gave alms generously to the people, and prayed to God always. About the ninth hour of the day he saw clearly in a vision an angel of God coming in and saying to him, "Cornelius!"*
>
> *And when he observed him, he was afraid, and said, "What is it, lord?"*
>
> *So he said to him, "Your prayers and your alms have come up for a memorial before God."*

The giving and prayers of Cornelius created a memorial before the Lord. It spoke in the Courts of Heaven and caused him to be remembered by God. Isaiah 43:26 tells us that when we put God in remembrance, we are presenting a case in His Courts.

> *Put Me in remembrance;*
> *Let us contend together;*

State your case, that you may be acquitted.

When there is something bringing God into remembrance concerning us, it is presenting evidence on our behalf. This is what Cornelius' offerings and prayers mingled together did. It created something in the heavenly realm that spoke before God and caused Him to remember this Gentile's house. We see this same principle in Numbers 10:10 where the people of God are commanded to blow the two silver trumpets over their offerings.

> *Also in the day of your gladness, in your appointed feasts, and at the beginning of your months, you shall blow the trumpets over your burnt offerings and over the sacrifices of your peace offerings; and they shall be a memorial for you before your God: I am the Lord your God.*

It wasn't enough that the people just brought their offerings; they had to blow these trumpets over them. Trumpets always speak of the declared word of God. Paul in speaking to the Corinthians about the spoken and declared word of God. First Corinthians 14:8 likens the prophetic to a trumpet sounding.

> *For if the trumpet makes an uncertain sound, who will prepare for battle?*

When the two trumpets were blown over the offerings, it was God telling us we must prophesy and pray over the offerings we bring. We must be like Cornelius. We need to mix our prayers and offerings together. It creates a memorial that speaks on our behalf before the Courts of Heaven and allows decisions to be rendered for us. It is appropriate that based on our giving we decree, petition, and request our needed breakthroughs to come. When we do this, it causes these things to begin to speak before the Courts and causes God to remember us. Remember, our money has a voice and gives testimony concerning us before the Lord. The Lord remembering Cornelius' house had great significance. As a result of the memorial speaking concerning him before God, God chose Cornelius' house above all other houses. There would have been literally myriads of Gentile houses in this day. However, God picked Cornelius' house as the one that the Holy Spirit would enter the Gentile world through. Up until this time, Christianity had been only within the Jewish world. When Cornelius obeys the angel's instructions to send for Peter to preach the gospel to him and his house, it was God using Cornelius' house as a gate to enter the Gentile world and culture. Acts 10:44-48 shows that as Peter spoke to the house of Cornelius, the Holy Spirit fell on these.

While Peter was still speaking these words, the Holy Spirit fell upon all those who heard the word. And those of the circumcision who believed were astonished, as many as came with Peter, because the gift of the Holy Spirit had been poured out on the Gentiles also. For they heard them speak with tongues and magnify God.

Then Peter answered, "Can anyone forbid water, that these should not be baptized who have received the Holy Spirit just as we have?" And he commanded them to be baptized in the name of the Lord. Then they asked him to stay a few days.

Cornelius' house was esteemed and chosen by God to be the portal the Holy Spirit came through into the Gentile world. This all happened because Cornelius' giving mixed with his prayers spoke before the Lord in His throne and Courts. Our money has a voice before God. I pray on a regular basis that my house would even be as Cornelius' house. I ask that my offerings and prayers would create a memorial speaking before God that would allow God to choose my house. I ask that my house could be a gate and portal that God could move through to touch the nations of the earth. This is what happened with Cornelius. May God esteem our houses before Him as well because of our giving mixed with our offerings that are speaking before His Courts.

> Lord, as we come before Your Courts, we ask that our money would have the right sound attached to it. Lord, we repent for any place we have held back our money on any level when we should have been honoring You with it. Forgive us, Lord, for this. We ask, Lord, that our finances would release a testimony before You that would cause You to remember our house as You remembered the house of Cornelius. Would You esteem our house and choose it for Your purposes in the earth. Would You allow Your blessings and life to flow in our house because of the testimony of our money speaking in Your Courts and causing You to remember us. Lord, we also ask that our tithe would connect us to Your present-day life on our behalf. Allow our tithe to declare before Your Courts that we believe You live. As this sound is heard before You, would You allow that which You are speaking on our behalf as our Intercessor to cause decisions to be rendered for us. Lord, we thank You for Your present-day life working for us and our connection to it because of the testimony of our tithe and our money. Remember

us, our God, for good based on our offering and
prayers presented before You. In Jesus' Name,
amen.

CHAPTER 9

THE VOICE
OF FIRST FRUITS

There are many different kinds of offerings that would speak on our behalf before the Lord. One of the main offerings is the First Fruits offering. Most people would connect a First Fruits offering with the tithe. They would consider this to be the same offering. However, this is incorrect. The tithe is what we bring to the Lord *after* our harvest. In other words, after we get paid, our finances come in, investments mature, houses sell, etc., we bring a tenth of that income to the Lord. We honor the Lord and Jesus as our High Priest after the Order of Melchizedek. As we saw in the last chapter, this testifies on our behalf and connects us to His present-day intercession and ministry on our behalf. The First Fruits offering, however, is different. The tithe is what we bring *after our harvest*, First Fruits are what we bring *before our harvest*. We can see clearly that First Fruits and tithes are two distinct offerings in Numbers 18 and also Nehemiah 10. Numbers

18:12 tells us that the First Fruits and the first portion of all things were given to Aaron as the high priest.

> *All the best of the oil, all the best of the new wine and the grain, their firstfruits which they offer to the Lord, I have given them to you.*

The First Fruits portion was designated to belong to the high priest for his service to the Lord and His people. The tithe went to the Levitical tribe who were appointed to serve with Aaron as the high priest and take care of the dwelling of God or the tabernacle/temple. Numbers 18:21 tells us this.

> *Behold, I have given the children of Levi all the tithes in Israel as an inheritance in return for the work which they perform, the work of the tabernacle of meeting.*

This means the First Fruits and the tithe were two separate offerings because they went to two separate groups of people. The high priest got the First Fruits while the Levites got the tithe to live from. This means clearly that First Fruits and tithes are two different offerings. As this principle transitions into the New Testament, we can see how it is to operate. The high priest in the Old Testament is a shadow of the apostle in the New. Hebrews 3:1 unveils this for us by linking the two terms together in the ministry of Jesus.

> *Therefore, holy brethren, partakers of the heavenly calling, consider the Apostle and High Priest of our confession, Christ Jesus.*

Jesus is both High Priest and Apostle. When we therefore read of the high priest in the Old Testament, we are reading of the apostle in the New Testament. So God's command to His people to bring First Fruits to the high priest/apostle was so through honor they could join, connect, and align with this authority He has appointed. Likewise, when the tithe is brought to honor the Levites, we are honoring those who have been appointed to guard, care, and keep the House of God. They speak of the pastoral ministry within the local church that cares for the people of God. God ordained through First Fruits and tithes that all these vital ministries would be cared for, but also that we as the people of God could connect with them through our strategic giving. Nehemiah 10:37 also points out that the First Fruits went to the high priest and his sons who were priests as well, while the tithes went to the Levites.

> *To bring the firstfruits of our dough, our offerings, the fruit from all kinds of trees, the new wine and oil, to*

*the priests, to the storerooms of the house of our God;
and to bring the tithes of our land to the Levites, for
the Levites should receive the tithes in all our farming
communities.*

So clearly First Fruits and tithes are separate and distinct offerings from each other. Some of the promises connected to First Fruits and tithes are similar. However, there are things we can gain from First Fruits that tithes will not produce because of what they are speaking and saying on our behalf.

This is how the Jewish people were taught to honor God with First Fruits. For instance, as their harvest would begin to ripen in the fields they would glean the first ripening heads of grain. The major part of the harvest was yet to mature. The first ripening grain, however, was gleaned and reaped and harvested. Leviticus 2:14-16 tells how the First Fruits offering of grain was to be offered and received.

*If you offer a grain offering of your firstfruits to the
Lord, you shall offer for the grain offering of your
firstfruits green heads of grain roasted on the fire,
grain beaten from full heads. And you shall put oil
on it, and lay frankincense on it. It is a grain offering. Then the priest shall burn the memorial portion:
part of its beaten grain and part of its oil, with all the
frankincense, as an offering made by fire to the Lord.*

Notice that the offering was *green heads of grain*. In other words, it was the *first portion* of the harvest that began to ripen. This portion was to be offered the Lord. It was to be given to the priest. The priest would take the *memorial portion* and burn it in fire. The memorial portion was a handful. Leviticus 2:2-3 shows that the memorial portion that was to be offered and presented to the Lord was this handful.

> *He shall bring it to Aaron's sons, the priests, one of whom shall take from it his handful of fine flour and oil with all the frankincense. And the priest shall burn it as a memorial on the altar, an offering made by fire, a sweet aroma to the Lord. The rest of the grain offering shall be Aaron's and his sons'. It is most holy of the offerings to the Lord made by fire.*

A handful was burnt before the Lord that created a *memorial* that spoke before the Lord on behalf of the one who brought the offering. This that was speaking created a memorial before God that caused them to be remembered. In other words, it spoke and gave testimony to the Lord of the one who brought the offering. The rest of the offering was for the livelihood of the priest. This was the way God provided for the priest from the offerings of the people. When the people brought the *First Fruits* of their harvest, or that which was the *first portion*, it spoke before the Lord and created this memorial.

As the First Fruits offering spoke before the Lord, it promised certain benefits to the one who honored God with it. To get a view of this, we need to understand what the First Fruit offering does. According to Romans 11:16, the First Fruits offering causes the *whole* or the *lump* to be holy to the Lord.

> *For if the firstfruit is holy, the lump is also holy; and*
> *if the root is holy, so are the branches.*

Paul is speaking this in regard to Israel and its place in the economy of God. Israel is the First Fruits of God. We as the Christian church *grew out of this root*. So we as the Gentile church are holy because we come from a holy root. The principle is valid in regard to how this occurs. In other words, when we take the first portion and offer it to God, it causes the *whole* that it came from to be holy as well. This is why First Fruits is so powerful. God doesn't ask us to give all. He does, however, ask to be honored with the first. When we take the first and best portion and honor Him with it, it causes that which it came from to be sanctified and holy as well. When something is *holy*, it means God treats it like it belongs to Him. It actually does, because it has been given to Him through the act and offering of First Fruits. Many times, people desire to give themselves, their marriage, children, business, or something else that is precious to them to God. They may even pray a prayer of dedication of this to the Lord. The real biblical way of *giving* something to the Lord, however, is through First Fruits. When I take the first and best portion of something and offer it to the Lord, the whole it came from is now dedicated to God. We see this idea in Ezekiel 44:30.

> *The best of all firstfruits of any kind, and every sacrifice of any kind from all your sacrifices, shall be the priest's; also you shall give to the priest the first of your ground meal, to cause a blessing to rest on your house.*

The Lord promised that when the first was given to the Lord from someone's house, it would *cause* a blessing to come on that house. In other words, when we dedicate our house to the Lord it allows the Lord the privilege and legal right to bless this house. Let's look at what this scripture is promising. First of all, it declares First Fruits *causes* something. This means nothing else can produce what First Fruits can produce. You can't wish it into place. You can't speak it into place. You can't think it into place. You can't even pray it into place. Only when we honor the Lord with the first and the best from our house is this *caused!* When something is caused, it means that something we did produced it. It didn't just happen, nor did it occur by accident. We set it in motion through our activity, desire, and obedience. We caused it. When we operate in First Fruits, we inaugurate something into operation. Something in the unseen realm begins to move on our behalf. This is the power of First Fruits.

A second thing this scripture declares is that the blessing comes to *rest*. This means it comes to stay. As I have lived life and ministered in the Body of Christ for decades now, I find many people beset with a sick heart. This is because of hope deferred. Proverbs 13:12 tells us what can happen when someone is disappointed time after time after time.

> *Hope deferred makes the heart sick,*
> *But when the desire comes, it is a tree of life.*

A sick heart is one that is no longer willing or perhaps able to believe. Most of the time, they are still functioning in appearance as good Christians. The problem is there is no vital faith in them. The years of disappointment have taken their toll and removed from them the ability or at least the willingness to believe. It is simply too big of a risk to again believe, only to have to endure the pain of disappointment again. They therefore shift into an emotional and spiritual place of just *doing life*, rather than being excited and adventurous concerning their destiny and future. Many times this has developed because of something that looked promising, only to see it dissipate and disappear. They got their hopes up only to have them dashed again. This is why the promise of the blessing *resting* on someone and something is so important. The Lord is promising that through First Fruits we can see something come and stay and not depart. It will last and be maintained on our life. The blessing will come to live with us and produce the goodness of God in our life. When we operate in First Fruits there is a voice that speaks on our behalf that causes us to be remembered by God. It will produce a lasting blessing that will not just be temporary but permanent upon our lives.

The third significant thing in this scripture is the blessing is on our *house*. When the Bible speaks of a house, it is not necessarily speaking of the structure we live in. The *house* is our family and lineage. God is promising that operating in First Fruits causes a lasting blessing to flow over our marriages, children, grandchildren, great-grandchildren, great-great-grandchildren, and generations to come. When we function in First Fruits, it is recorded in Heaven and speaks for us and our generations to come. It secures the blessings of God over all that is dear to us. This is actually what the widow of Zarephath did when she gave her last bread to the prophet Elijah in First Kings 17:12-15. The widow was making her and her son's last meal when she encountered the prophet. By her own admission they were going to eat it and die. However, when the prophet confronted her, he pushed her into the First Fruits principle. This unlocked a new future for her and her family.

> So she said, "As the Lord your God lives, I do not have bread, only a handful of flour in a bin, and a little oil in a jar; and see, I am gathering a couple of sticks that I may go in and prepare it for myself and my son, that we may eat it, and die."
>
> And Elijah said to her, "Do not fear; go and do as you have said, but make me a small cake from it first, and bring it to me; and afterward make some for yourself and your son. For thus says the Lord God of Israel: 'The bin of flour shall not be used up, nor shall the jar of oil run dry, until the day the Lord sends rain on the earth.'"
>
> So she went away and did according to the word of Elijah; and she and he and her household ate for many days.

What a story! As a result of her willingness to hear and obey the word of the Lord, she and her family survived the famine and knew the goodness of God. What released this for her that others didn't get? It was First Fruits and it was speaking on her behalf before the Lord. Notice the woman declares she is preparing *her last.* The prophet tells her to make him one *first*. He was saying to her, "*Take your last, turn it into your first, and get a miracle.*" This is exactly what she did. Notice that the promise of the prophet was "if you will honor God in me and through me by giving me a cake first, you will have an *afterward*." She had already said she didn't have a future. She had just said they were going to eat this last, then die. The prophet is promising her, on the basis of First Fruits, that a blessing will rest on her house. Instead of her and her son dying, they would have an afterward / future. This is the power of First Fruits speaking on our behalf before the Lord. It puts a blessing on us and our lineage for generations to come. Through its voice it provides for us a future and a destiny.

Proverbs 3:9-10 (Reserved Standard Version) shows us a direct connection between First Fruits and prosperity. When we function in First Fruits it releases many different dimensions of blessings for us. Financial blessing, increase, wealth, and riches is one of them.

> *Honor the Lord with your substance*
> *and with the first fruits of all your produce;*
> *then your barns will be filled with plenty,*
> *and your vats will be bursting with wine.*

When we step into the realm of First Fruits and honor God, it produces these new levels of prosperity. We are promised barns filled with plenty and vats overflowing with wine. One of the main businesses of the Jewish people in Bible days was agriculture. When God promises filled barns and overflowing vats of wine, this means prosperity. It means He was going to place on their business a blessing that would produce abundantly. Notice that barns and vats are in the plural. This means that the harvest would be so significant that it would require multiple facilities to contain it. This is the heart of God. However, it is clear that this is connected to operating in First Fruits. When we take our first and our best and bring it to the Lord, it speaks on our behalf and allows this kind of blessing to flow. We know this because of Deuteronomy 26:15-19. In these verses and the previous ones, God is laying down the principles governing First Fruits and tithes. He is promising the children of Israel that when they operate in this principle it will speak before Him and allow the blessings to flow over them.

> Look down from Your holy habitation, from heaven, and bless Your people Israel and the land which You have given us, just as You swore to our fathers, "a land flowing with milk and honey."
>
> This day the Lord your God commands you to observe these statutes and judgments; therefore you shall be careful to observe them with all your heart and with

all your soul. Today you have proclaimed the Lord to be your God, and that you will walk in His ways and keep His statutes, His commandments, and His judgments, and that you will obey His voice. Also today the Lord has proclaimed you to be His special people, just as He promised you, that you should keep all His commandments, and that He will set you high above all nations which He has made, in praise, in name, and in honor, and that you may be a holy people to the Lord your God, just as He has spoken.

Notice that as they operated in this principle they could then pray prayers asking for certain blessings to flow. They are requesting for God to look upon them from Heaven and bless them. Notice, however, that God speaks of *today*. He says that through their First Fruits and tithes they are *saying something*. They *proclaimed* with their giving a proclamation and testimony before the Lord. This is because their First Fruits were speaking for them. As a result of what their offering was saying, God responded back with a decision on their behalf. He says *also today*, "I'm going to bless you. I'm going to declare you a special people and will set you and promote you on high before the nations." God makes powerful promises and decrees over Israel based on what their offerings of First Fruits and tithes are speaking. In other words, God is releasing a decision based on the testimony and voice of their First Fruits offering and tithes.

We too should operate in First Fruits and tithes. When we do, there is a testimony speaking for us before the Lord. It is giving Him the needed judicial activity on our behalf that allows His blessing, prosperity, and goodness to be seen in us. He is able to give us a name/reputation. This means people will know us and think good of us. He will give us praise or call attention to us. Where we might have been unnoticed, people become aware of us. He will grant us honor. This speaks of being set in places of influence and even authority and power. He also promises that we will be holy to Him. In other words, He will arise and defend us because we are His people. These are just some of the promises connected to First Fruits. This principle is a critical piece to coming into the prosperity and wealth the Lord desires for us. May we prayerfully step into this principle and release the voice that will speak for us in His Courts. Decisions will be rendered that allow a new place of life and even riches for us!

Lord, as I bring my First Fruits before You, I ask that it would speak on my behalf and cause You to remember me. This which my offering is speaking—cause it to allow a blessing to rest on my house. Arise and defend me, Lord, on the basis of this which my First Fruits is saying. I thank You that my house, business, ministry, and all aspects of my life are now given to You through my First Fruits offering. I thank You that You now treat it as belonging to You because they have been given to You through First Fruits. Thank You, Lord, that according to Your word my barns are filled with plenty and my vats overflow with new wine. Prosperity is unlocked for me because of my First Fruits offered before You, in Jesus' Name, amen.

CHAPTER 10

RESTRAINING ORDERS AGAINST THE DEVIL

The obtaining of wealth, prosperity, and riches can have several sources. In the book of Job we can see that God set restraining orders against the devil, allowing Job and his family to prosper. When we think about Job, we almost always consider the trouble he went through. However, before he went through his tribulation and after it was over, Job was a tremendously prosperous man. He was said to be the greatest and wealthiest man of his time. It could be said he was the Bill Gates or Warren Buffet of his day. Job 1:1-3 details Job's wealth and the way God had blessed him.

> There was a man in the land of Uz, whose name was Job; and that man was blameless and upright, and one who feared God and shunned evil. And seven sons and three daughters were born to him. Also, his possessions were seven thousand sheep, three

> *thousand camels, five hundred yoke of oxen, five hun-*
> *dred female donkeys, and a very large household, so*
> *that this man was the greatest of all the people of the*
> *East.*

Job's wealth had granted him great realms of influence and reputation. He was honored and esteemed as a man of authority and significance. The Bible actually gives us some insight into what had allowed Job to have this kind of wealth and placement. We should pay attention to this in that it can give us understanding for our own lives. When Satan is summoned before God's Court to give an account of where he has been and what he has been doing, God brings Job up. Job 1:6-12 shows the discourse between God and Satan that caused what happened to Job to occur. This would have been in the spiritual unseen realm. Job would have had no awareness of it. We must realize that so much of what occurs in our lives can have roots in something transpiring in the unseen world. It might have seemed to Job that it was circumstantial or just bad luck. However, it was *caused* by a case being presented by Satan against him.

> *Now there was a day when the sons of God came*
> *to present themselves before the Lord, and Satan*
> *also came among them. And the Lord said to Satan,*
> *"From where do you come?"*

So Satan answered the Lord and said, "From going to and fro on the earth, and from walking back and forth on it."

Then the Lord said to Satan, "Have you considered My servant Job, that there is none like him on the earth, a blameless and upright man, one who fears God and shuns evil?"

So Satan answered the Lord and said, "Does Job fear God for nothing? Have You not made a hedge around him, around his household, and around all that he has on every side? You have blessed the work of his hands, and his possessions have increased in the land. But now, stretch out Your hand and touch all that he has, and he will surely curse You to Your face!"

And the Lord said to Satan, "Behold, all that he has is in your power; only do not lay a hand on his person."

So Satan went out from the presence of the Lord.

We can focus in on what allowed this case against Job that produced the tragedies. Let me just say it is my opinion it was because of that which his offerings were speaking. Notice that the accusation of Satan was that Job was not serving God with a pure heart. He accused him of only serving God because of how much God had blessed him. No one can bring an accusation against another in a court of law unless they produce evidence to back it up. What was the evidence Satan had against Job? It was the offerings Job had brought on behalf of his children. When his children would have parties, he was afraid they had cursed God. In his effort to stop God from judging them, Job would bring an offering to *appease* God. We see this in Job 1:4-5.

> And his sons would go and feast in their houses, each on his appointed day, and would send and invite their three sisters to eat and drink with them. So it was, when the days of feasting had run their course, that Job would send and sanctify them, and he would rise early in the morning and offer burnt offerings according to the number of them all. For Job said, "It may be that my sons have sinned and cursed God in their hearts." Thus Job did regularly.

This religious activity was not done in a spirit of faith toward the Lord but rather fear. We know this because in Job 3:25, when the tragedies began to come against Job, he declared what he feared had now come on him.

> For the thing I greatly feared has come upon me,
> And what I dreaded has happened to me.

As much as Job loved and honored God, there was an element of fear ruling his life. The offerings he brought on behalf of his children were not faith offerings. They were offerings laced with fear. Remember in a previous chapter we showed that our offerings speak. Whatever the state of our heart is when we bring our offering is what it is saying concerning us. When Job brought offerings to try and secure his children from harm, the devil took the testimony of fear attached to them and used it to bring an accusation of impure motives before the Lord. This was the evidence Satan presented to bring his accusation. Our offerings are always to be offerings of worship, adoration, faith, and even hilarity. Second Corinthians 9:7 shows that our offerings must not be grudging or with a wrong motive. They must be from a right heart of love and devotion.

> *So let each one give as he purposes in his heart, not grudgingly or of necessity; for God loves a cheerful giver.*

The word *cheerful* is the Greek word *hilaros*. It means "to be merry, prompt, and willing." It is the word we get our English word *hilarious* from. Our offerings are to be filled with the joy of the Lord and excitement about honoring Him. This was not the attitude in the offerings of Job. His offerings were filled with fear and probably even manipulation. The devil used this against him as evidence of an impure heart in serving God. If we have ever given to the Lord out of an impure heart, we should come before the Courts of Heaven and ask that this offering's sound be annulled. We should ask for the blood of Jesus to speak for us and revoke the devil's rights to use this as evidence (see Hebrews 12:24). When we do, the Judge of the whole earth will render a verdict and decision on our behalf.

Even though Job went through the terrible things he did, it doesn't remove the other secrets we see in and from his life. Prior to his troubles and after them, the blessing of God was great on Job. What allowed this was a restraining/protective order set by God on his behalf. When Satan brought the case against him, it caused this legal statute to be removed. It was there, though, beforehand and after the trials. What was it that allowed this to occur?

First of all, let's see this restraining/protective order in place. The Bible says there was a *hedge* about Job. This is the Hebrew word *suwk*. This word means "to be shut in, a restraint and protection." Clearly this wasn't some formation in the spirit world that wouldn't allow Satan physically to come close to Job. It was something legal in place that forbade the demonic any access to Job and his family. It was a restraining/protective order from the Courts of Heaven. In natural courts in earth, judges set in place restraining/protective orders that do not allow threatening people to come close to others. Should they violate the restraining order, they can be arrested and placed in jail and confinement. For instance, the restraining/ protective order may declare the threatening individual is forbidden to come within 100 feet of the person the order is protecting. Should they do this, they have violated the court order and the police and authorities can arrest and remove them. This is what was in place over Job and his family. Please notice this restraining/protective order over Job provided him with protection for his family, great realms of influence, *and* an environment in which he greatly prospered. As long as this restraining order was in place against the devil, he had no power to devour Job or anything he had. This allowed a life of bliss, blessing, and prosperity. However, once the restraining/protective order was removed, everything including his wealth was devoured. We see this in Job 1:12-17 when, it appears, the wealth of Job was taken away in a few moments.

> *And the Lord said to Satan, "Behold, all that he has is in your power; only do not lay a hand on his person."*
>
> *So Satan went out from the presence of the Lord. Now there was a day when his sons and daughters were eating and drinking wine in their oldest brother's house; and a messenger came to Job and said, "The oxen were plowing and the donkeys feeding*

beside them, when the Sabeans raided them and took them away—indeed they have killed the servants with the edge of the sword; and I alone have escaped to tell you!"

While he was still speaking, another also came and said, "The fire of God fell from heaven and burned up the sheep and the servants, and consumed them; and I alone have escaped to tell you!"

While he was still speaking, another also came and said, "The Chaldeans formed three bands, raided the camels and took them away, yes, and killed the servants with the edge of the sword; and I alone have escaped to tell you!"

When God agreed to lift the restraining/protective order based on the case Satan had presented, the wealth of Job was lost. We also know his children died and then later Job himself was afflicted with sickness and disease. All of this was because of the lifting of the restraining/protective order from the Courts of Heaven. This gave Satan access to Job that he previously didn't have. Our focus is on the wealth that Job lost. As long as the restraint of God was against Satan, Job prospered and increased in his wealth. The moment the restraint was removed, the wealth and all that was valuable to Job was lost. There was a reason, however, for why the restraining/protective order from Heaven was in place. It was because of the testimony of God Himself concerning Job. God Himself bore witness to Job. This allowed this restraining order to be in place. We may have others testify of us, which is good. However, when God Himself testifies of us, it is something that is set and established. Let me draw your attention to Job 1:8. This verse shows God bearing witness to Job. His own testimony concerning Job allowed this restraining/protective order to be in place that produced the prosperity he enjoyed.

> *Then the Lord said to Satan, "Have you considered My servant Job, that there is none like him on the earth, a blameless and upright man, one who fears God and shuns evil?"*

These statements of the Lord in His own Court concerning Job set the restraining/protective order in place that caused the environment and atmosphere that allowed Job to prosper and increase. If we desire to see this kind of prosperity, we should also endeavor to see these restraining/protective orders set in place.

Before I show us the things that God testified of Job that allowed this, let me show you the two other places where I see God Himself testifying concerning people and the results of it. The first one is Abel in Hebrews 11:4.

> *By faith Abel offered to God a more excellent sacri-*
> *fice than Cain, through which he obtained witness*
> *that he was righteous, God testifying of his gifts; and*
> *through it he being dead still speaks.*

Notice that Abel obtained *witness* that he was righteous because God *testified* of the gifts he brought. Both the word *witness* and the word *testifying* in this scripture are the Greek word *martureo*. It means "to be a witness and give evidence." It is a judicial word. Based on the excellent sacrifice that Abel brought, God Himself testifies on his behalf. As a result of the Lord Himself giving judicial testimony of Abel and his offering, Abel is still speaking today. This can mean we are still learning lessons today from his life and/or it can mean that Abel obtained a place in the Cloud of Witnesses that is still allowing him influence today from Heaven (see Hebrews 12:1). Regardless, the point is that God testifying of the offering of Abel has granted Abel a place before the Lord of great influence and effect.

A second place I see God testifying is in Malachi 3:4-5. God proclaims that on the basis of an offering that is accepted, He will become a swift witness.

> *"Then the offering of Judah and Jerusalem*
> *Will be pleasant to the Lord,*

As in the days of old,

As in former years.

And I will come near you for judgment;

I will be a swift witness

Against sorcerers,

Against adulterers,

Against perjurers,

Against those who exploit wage earners and widows
and orphans,

And against those who turn away an alien—

Because they do not fear Me,"

Says the Lord of hosts.

God promises to swiftly testify against the atrocities that are afflicting society when we bring an offering in righteousness. The word *witness* here in the Hebrew is *ed.* It means "a witness and a testimony." The main point we should see here is that God Himself will testify judicially concerning the matter. This is powerful. It's one thing when men testify. It's another thing when angels testify. It's something when the Cloud of Witnesses testifies and/or the blood speaks. However, this is declaring that God Himself will testify and speak concerning us and our matters. When God Himself testifies, it is a certain and done deal. This is what happened to Job. God Himself testified on Job's behalf. The result was a restraining/protective order set in place that brought safety, influence, and great prosperity. The devil had no right or ability to afflict, devour, or destroy Job. Job became the greatest man of the East because of this. What was the testimony of God concerning Job that allowed and produced this?

There are six things God testified of Job that caused this restraining/protective order of God to be put into place. Again, Job 1:8 unveils these six things.

> Then the Lord said to Satan, "Have you considered My servant Job, that there is none like him on the earth, a blameless and upright man, one who fears God and shuns evil?"

God first testifies that Job is His servant. The word *servant* is the Hebrew word *ebed*. It means "a bond servant." In Hebrew culture and law, someone became a bond slave when they chose to stay in a master's house and not go free. This was of their own volition and desire. Deuteronomy 15:12-17 gives insight to the process of becoming a bond slave.

> If your brother, a Hebrew man, or a Hebrew woman, is sold to you and serves you six years, then in the seventh year you shall let him go free from you. And when you send him away free from you, you shall

not let him go away empty-handed; you shall supply him liberally from your flock, from your threshing floor, and from your winepress. From what the Lord your God has blessed you with, you shall give to him. You shall remember that you were a slave in the land of Egypt, and the Lord your God redeemed you; therefore I command you this thing today. And if it happens that he says to you, "I will not go away from you," because he loves you and your house, since he prospers with you, then you shall take an awl and thrust it through his ear to the door, and he shall be your servant forever. Also to your female servant you shall do likewise.

A person in Hebrew culture could sell themselves into slavery and serve for six years to be freed from a debt. If, however, over the six years of slavery they fall in love with the master and his house, they could request to be a bond slave. This would declare they would not go out as a free person again. They would voluntarily revoke their freedom for the love of their master and his house. This is a picture of what happens to us as we serve the Lord. We originally came to the Lord to escape our debt we could not pay. We needed another to free us and forgive us of that debt. As we serve the Lord, though, we fall in love with Him and desire to not go away. His love and the love of His house changes our hearts. We choose to become

His bond slave. This is what happened to Job. He was the bond slave of the Lord. This was the testimony of God concerning Job. He had chosen to not go out free but to be God's servant forever.

The second thing God testified of Job was *there was none like him.* This means that Job lived an uncommon life most would not choose. He would do in faith what others wouldn't do. We see Jesus referring to the widow of Zarephath and Naaman the leper in this category as He spoke to the unbelief of Nazareth, His hometown. Luke 4:25-27 shows the people chiding Jesus and wanting to see miracles like He had done in other places. Jesus' response was that only those who showed real faith would partake of and witness such things.

> *But I tell you truly, many widows were in Israel in the days of Elijah, when the heaven was shut up three years and six months, and there was a great famine throughout all the land; but to none of them was Elijah sent except to Zarephath, in the region of Sidon, to a woman who was a widow. And many lepers were in Israel in the time of Elisha the prophet, and none of them was cleansed except Naaman the Syrian.*

Jesus shows that it wasn't the need God responded to; it was faith. There were many widows and many lepers.

Only these two had God move for them. The reason why was they did what others wouldn't do. They therefore got what others didn't get. This was what set Job apart and caused God to testify of him. There was none like him. May we be of this spirit and heart as well, that would allow God to speak concerning us also.

The third thing God testified of Job was he was *blameless*. This is the Hebrew word *tam*. It means "to be undefiled." It also means "to be coupled together." When God testified that Job was blameless, He was declaring he was *coupled together* with the Lord. They were walking in union with each other. This speaks of intimacy and closeness of fellowship. The intimacy that Job had with God produced a life of being undefiled before Him. The Lord spoke to me a few years ago and said, "*Every time you say no to the flesh, you are saying I love You more.*" I believe this is the way the Lord sees our devotion to Him. We are coupled together with the Lord.

The fourth quality that God testified of Job was he was *upright*. This is the Hebrew word *yashar*. It means "to be straight, full of equity, and righteous." This means we deal righteously with people. We are just and fair. We aren't trying to take advantage of someone else. We aren't a *Jacob* who was a *heel grabber*. This is referring to when Jacob was born and he reached and grabbed the heel of his twin brother Esau who was born before him. They named him

Jacob as a result (see Genesis 25:26). The Lord had to in finality meet Jacob and deal with this nature of deceiving, manipulating, and supplanting people to get ahead. This happened in Genesis 32:24-28.

> *Then Jacob was left alone; and a Man wrestled with him until the breaking of day. Now when He saw that He did not prevail against him, He touched the socket of his hip; and the socket of Jacob's hip was out of joint as He wrestled with him. And He said, "Let Me go, for the day breaks."*
>
> *But he said, "I will not let You go unless You bless me!"*
>
> *So He said to him, "What is your name?"*
>
> *He said, "Jacob."*
>
> *And He said, "Your name shall no longer be called Jacob, but Israel; for you have struggled with God and with men, and have prevailed."*

As a result of an all-night wrestling match with God represented by His angel, Jacob was changed to Israel. *Israel* means in the Hebrew *he will rule as God.* We all have to go through this process. We all have a *Jacob* in us. If we can allow the Lord to *wrestle* this nature from us, we can become those who *rule with God and even as God* as His representatives. Job was of this nature. He was upright, having dealt with the nature of Jacob within him. God testified of this on his behalf.

A fifth thing God spoke of Job was he *feared God*. Fearing God has so many aspects connected to it. Fearing God is not something that is tormenting. Fearing God is having an awareness that if I serve and obey Him, things will go well in my life. I also know if I disobey Him things will work against me in my life. This causes me to walk in fear and trembling before Him and to seek to always please Him. Hebrews 12:28-29 tells us that we should serve God reverentially and in the fear of the Lord.

> *Therefore, since we are receiving a kingdom which cannot be shaken, let us have grace, by which we may serve God acceptably with reverence and godly fear. For our God is a consuming fire.*

Out of the fear of the Lord, we are aware everything will be tested by fire. There will be a day when all my works will be tested by my God who is a consuming fire. Paul speaks of this in First Corinthians 3:13-15.

> *Each one's work will become clear; for the Day will declare it, because it will be revealed by fire; and the fire will test each one's work, of what sort it is. If anyone's work which he has built on it endures, he will receive a reward. If anyone's work is burned, he*

*will suffer loss; but he himself will be saved, yet so as
through fire.*

We are told that when we stand before the Lord our
works will be tried by the fire of who God is. Everything
will be made clear on that day. Notice this isn't about getting to Heaven. It is about the reward we will or will not
have. This is what Hebrews is saying. We are to live our life
in such a way that we are aware everything will be tested
by this fire. I am to serve the Lord out of this fear knowing
my works will be manifested. From the fear of the Lord,
we would not suffer loss but we would be granted a good
reward in the time to come. This is the fear of the Lord for
the believer. Job walked in this and God testified of him
concerning it.

The sixth and final thing God spoke concerning Job
was he *shunned evil*. This is the Hebrew word *cuwr*. It
means "to decline, depart, remove, or pluck away." When
I read this, I think of Jesus' words concerning dealing with
things that would work against eternal life. Matthew 5:28-
30 reveals Jesus speaking strong words about dealing with
sin and uncleanness in our lives.

*But I say to you that whoever looks at a woman to
lust for her has already committed adultery with her
in his heart. If your right eye causes you to sin, pluck
it out and cast it from you; for it is more profitable for*

you that one of your members perish, than for your whole body to be cast into hell. And if your right hand causes you to sin, cut it off and cast it from you; for it is more profitable for you that one of your members perish, than for your whole body to be cast into hell.

Clearly Jesus is not saying we should physically mutilate ourselves. He is saying, however, that we should not give place to sin in our lives. The basic gist is that we must *aggressively deal* with sin and unrighteousness. We cannot just give room to it. We must repent and turn from that which would fight against God's purposes. We need the grace of God for this. This was what Job did in shunning evil. God testified of this concerning him. Job was one who fled evil and pursued righteousness. May it be so for us as well.

The result of these six testimonies of God for Job was that a restraint against the powers of darkness was set. Behind this restraint, blessing, bliss, and prosperity were unleashed. So it can be for us as well. God desires and needs for us to prosper. The result will be us living a life that depicts the goodness of God and also allows His desires to be seen in the earth.

Lord, as I come before Your Courts, I repent for all places where I have not walked according to Your word. I ask, Lord, that You would set in place a restraining/protective order on my behalf. I ask that the devil would be forbidden by this order to come close to me or what concerns me. I ask that because of this restraining/protective order all I love would be guarded and secured. I ask that You would grant me influence. I ask that an atmosphere and environment would be created from this restraining/protective order that would allow prosperity, wealth, increase, and riches to be secured. Lord, would You please testify of me that I am Your bond servant, that I walk an uncommon life, that I am blameless, upright, fear the Lord, and that I shun evil. As a result of this, Your testimony concerning me, I ask for this restraining/protective order to be set in place that would allow me prosperity on every level. In Jesus' Name, amen.

CHAPTER 11

RESETTING TIME

One of the chief tactics of the devil against us and our prosperity is to disrupt the timing of God. We see in Daniel 7:25-26 that the devil through the Anti-Christ spirit would intend to change times and laws. This can mean several different things. However, at its core we can understand that the devil interferes with *when* things are supposed to occur in the timetable of God.

He shall speak pompous words against the Most High,

Shall persecute the saints of the Most High,

And shall intend to change times and law.

Then the saints shall be given into his hand

For a time and times and half a time.

But the court shall be seated,

And they shall take away his dominion,

To consume and destroy it forever.

If the devil can successfully stop something from happening when it is ordained, then he can throw things out of order. In regard to prosperity, we can then see this interrupted and disturbed. We see the devil messing with timing in different places in scripture. One is when the children of Israel were supposed to leave the bondage of Egypt. Originally God had said to Abraham that his descendants would be in captivity for 400 years. This is revealed in Genesis 15:13.

> Then He said to Abram: "Know certainly that your descendants will be strangers in a land that is not theirs, and will serve them, and they will afflict them four hundred years."

Clearly God set their servitude in Egypt at 400 years. Yet when they finally are delivered from Egypt it was in the 430th year. We see this in Exodus 12:40-41.

> Now the sojourn of the children of Israel who lived in Egypt was four hundred and thirty years. And it came to pass at the end of the four hundred and thirty years—on that very same day—it came to pass that all the armies of the Lord went out from the land of Egypt.

Was God speaking in generalities when He said 400 years, or did something lengthen their time in captivity? I think it is clear that it was expanded. The devil was able through his maneuvering to cause what God intended to not happen on time. The result was 30 more years of poverty, hardship, cruelty, lack, and need. How often has this happened to the people of God? As a result of the devil successfully manipulating time, we stay in a place less than the blessing of God. Our prosperity does not come. The result is a hopelessness that saps the very expectation of God from our life. The good news is, God is able to reset timing.

Another place where we see the devil disrupting the timing of God is when the Jews were sent back from Babylonian captivity to rebuild the temple, Jerusalem, and the nation of Israel. In Haggai 1:2-7, we see the prophet challenging the people of God who were sent back to rebuild. However, they have gotten sidetracked from the intent of God. The building has been on hiatus for around 17 years. The devil has disrupted timing again. Notice what has happened.

> *"Thus speaks the Lord of hosts, saying: 'This people says, "The time has not come, the time that the Lord's house should be built."'"*

> *Then the word of the Lord came by Haggai the prophet, saying, "Is it time for you yourselves to dwell in your paneled houses, and this temple to lie in ruins?" Now therefore, thus says the Lord of hosts: "Consider your ways!*
>
> *You have sown much, and bring in little;*
>
> *You eat, but do not have enough;*
>
> *You drink, but you are not filled with drink;*
>
> *You clothe yourselves, but no one is warm;*
>
> *And he who earns wages,*
>
> *Earns wages to put into a bag with holes."*
>
> *Thus says the Lord of hosts: "Consider your ways!"*

The people had gotten in agreement with the disrupted timing. They were saying it wasn't time to rebuild. Notice that because of this poverty, lack, and need are overtaking them. They sow much but get a little harvest. They drink but are not satisfied. They clothe themselves but aren't comfortable. They earn money but it doesn't go far enough. This is a result of them being out of the timing of God and not in agreement with what they should be doing. This is what occurs when the timing of God is interrupted. We must appeal to the Court of Heaven to have it reset. This is what happened in Daniel 7. The Court was seated and the rights the enemy was claiming to mess with

God's perfect timing were revoked. The way we begin to present our case before the Courts of Heaven to see timing set back into order is with repentance. We must repent for any place we have come into agreement with the interruptions of the Lord. God is declaring to the people in Haggai to *consider your ways!* In other words, take inventory of what is happening and repent and make the adjustments necessary. When we do this, we can then appeal to the Courts and ask for the blessings and prosperity of the Lord to flow. We may have to repent for stubbornness. We may have to repent for choosing our own ways. We may have to repent for bad and unwise decisions. We may have to repent for seeking our own stuff first rather than putting God's things first.

This was what the people in the book of Haggai were doing. Instead of building the house of God, they were building their own houses ahead of God's. This was altering the timetable of God. The result was lack and need. As we repent, the timing of God can be reset and the prosperity of God come again. We see this promised in Joel 2:17-26. As we turn our hearts back to God and repent for any place we have agreed with the devil and his disruptions, great blessings and prosperity begin to flow. Look at what God promises.

Let the priests, who minister to the Lord,

Weep between the porch and the altar;

Let them say, "Spare Your people, O Lord,

And do not give Your heritage to reproach,

That the nations should rule over them.

Why should they say among the peoples,

'Where is their God?'"

Then the Lord will be zealous for His land,

And pity His people.

The Lord will answer and say to His people,

"Behold, I will send you grain and new wine and oil,

And you will be satisfied by them;

I will no longer make you a reproach among the nations.

But I will remove far from you the northern army,

And will drive him away into a barren and desolate land,

With his face toward the eastern sea

And his back toward the western sea;

His stench will come up,

And his foul odor will rise,

Because he has done monstrous things."

Fear not, O land;

Be glad and rejoice,

For the Lord has done marvelous things!

Do not be afraid, you beasts of the field;

For the open pastures are springing up,

And the tree bears its fruit;

The fig tree and the vine yield their strength.

Be glad then, you children of Zion,

And rejoice in the Lord your God;

For He has given you the former rain faithfully,

And He will cause the rain to come down for you—

The former rain,

And the latter rain in the first month.

The threshing floors shall be full of wheat,

And the vats shall overflow with new wine and oil.

So I will restore to you the years that the swarming
locust has eaten,

The crawling locust,

The consuming locust,

And the chewing locust,

My great army which I sent among you.

You shall eat in plenty and be satisfied,

And praise the name of the Lord your God,

Who has dealt wondrously with you;

And My people shall never be put to shame.

Notice the promise of God as they repented—to send grain, new wine, and oil. The army of locusts and other creatures that devoured their harvest would be driven away. The fig tree and vine would yield their strength. The former and latter rains to bring in an abundant harvest would come. Threshing floors would be full of wheat and vats would overflow with new wine and oil. All of this is language promising a turning of fortunes and a producing of great wealth and prosperity. Notice that this occurs because of a resetting of time. God promises to *restore the years that were eaten up!* This means that the productivity of the years that were devoured will be replenished. The literal years obviously cannot be brought back, but the productivity of those years can. In other words, God is promising an acceleration of harvest and wealth as timing is reset! All that was lost in previous years will be restored in a short-term fashion.

Mary and I have watched this happen in our lives. Through different circumstances and the unscrupulous behavior of people I trusted, Mary and I lost much. What I thought I had set in place for our future was taken away and destroyed. We ended up with only what we had and needed for the moment. As most people would have had things in place for their latter years, we found ourselves with a very uncertain future. In the midst of this there were people prophesying restoration and replenishment to us. It seemed in the natural not to be possible. I then discovered the Courts of Heaven and the idea of resetting timing. As we went into the Courts and dealt with the accusations of the devil against us, God reset timing on our behalf. The devourer was rebuked and revoked and the acceleration of the blessing of God was set into place. We have literally seen an amazing release of wealth come in a small amount of time. We have seen God's promised restoration materialize. We no longer are uncertain about the future. God's word and His Courts have been faithful.

Leviticus 25:19-22 shows how God would accelerate harvest and prosperity during the time when the land rested every seven years.

> *Then the land will yield its fruit, and you will eat your fill, and dwell there in safety.*
>
> *And if you say, "What shall we eat in the seventh year, since we shall not sow nor gather in our produce?" Then I will command My blessing on you in the sixth year, and it will bring forth produce enough for three years. And you shall sow in the eighth year, and eat old produce until the ninth year; until its produce comes in, you shall eat of the old harvest.*

God promised that if they obeyed Him and gave the land a Sabbath's rest and did not plant it on the seventh year, He would bless the harvest of the sixth year. In one year, the land would produce three years' worth of harvest. I am pointing this out to show us that God is capable of great acceleration of prosperity when we obey Him and honor His ways.

If you feel that things have been disrupted by the devil and the timing of the Lord has been thwarted, we can deal with this in the Courts of Heaven. If you have been stolen from and suffered loss, the Court of Heaven can rearrange this. We can ask for a resetting of the timing of God and the reinstituting of His purposes. We can petition the Courts and see God render decisions that restore the blessing of God and bring us back into the wealth, riches, and prosperity of the Lord. It is His passion for you!

Lord, as I come before Your Courts, I sense the devil has disrupted the timing of God in my life. I am sure that things have gotten out of the order of what God intended. I repent for all places I have agreed with this through any stubbornness, rebellion, unwise decisions, and choices I have made. I ask, Lord, that Your blood would speak for me and that I would be forgiven. Lord, would You revoke all legal rights the devil is claiming to hold me in lack, need, and even poverty. I ask You that these bondages would be broken and the snare undone. I also ask, Lord, for the favor of the Lord to now come on me. I ask for open doors of blessing to manifest. I ask, Lord, not only for prosperity to come but for an acceleration of it in my life. Lord, open my heart to discern Your ways. Make me sensitive to Your voice that I might move in agreement with You and Your timing. Thank You so much, Lord, for mercy from Your Courts, the breaking of every spirit of poverty, and the establishment of wealth in my life. In Jesus' Name, amen.

CHAPTER 12

RICH TOWARD GOD

When we study the scriptures, it becomes very clear that God desires His people to prosper. Yet in the midst of this, either from scandalous intent or pure motives, sometimes we have seen things get *out of balance*. My pastor in training me to handle the Word of God would say to me, "*God loves a just balance.*" He was seeking to make sure I didn't teeter away from the tension of opposing views. In scripture we see this in many different areas, including the realm surrounding money, finance, and prosperity. Paul told his spiritual son Timothy that he should be careful to properly dissect the word of God in Second Timothy 2:15.

> *Be diligent to present yourself approved to God, a worker who does not need to be ashamed, rightly dividing the word of truth.*

In many cases in scripture, for every truth there is an opposing truth that holds it in balance. To embrace a truth to the *exclusion* of another truth is to end up in error and even deceit. This is true concerning prosperity. With this being said, I want to clearly proclaim that I believe in the gospel that produces prosperity. The term *prosperity gospel* has been coined to denigrate and seek to discredit those who believe God would have us to prosper. I believe God's heart is for us to prosper with every part of my being. Who would want to serve a God who barely takes care of His children, if at all? Even David declared in the famous Psalm 23:1 that we will not want when God is our shepherd.

The Lord is my shepherd; I shall not want.

David is declaring a strong confidence toward God that He will not only meet his needs, but satisfy him also with his wants! God is a good God who desires His children's wellbeing. Psalm 34:10 says that whoever seeks the Lord will be blessed with *good things*.

The young lions lack and suffer hunger;
But those who seek the Lord shall not lack any good
thing.

Young lions are those whose confidence is in their own strength and power. They believe they are strong enough themselves to see sufficiency manifest. However, the scripture is declaring that the real source of good things and our securing of them is from God and our seeking of Him. When we make Him our source and our hope, He will not fail us. He will, in fact, see to it that our confidence in Him is rewarded with these *good things.* He is such a kind and benevolent Father who loves us much and desires our prosperity.

With this said, we cannot ignore other scriptures. There are times when we see God's people serving Him faithfully and yet being in need and even want. Let's examine this to *rightly divide the word of truth.* Revelation 2:9-10 shows us that the church at Smyrna was in a place of poverty. Jesus actually is commending them in this present state.

> *I know your works, tribulation, and poverty (but you are rich); and I know the blasphemy of those who say they are Jews and are not, but are a synagogue of Satan. Do not fear any of those things which you are about to suffer. Indeed, the devil is about to throw some of you into prison, that you may be tested, and you will have tribulation ten days. Be faithful until death, and I will give you the crown of life.*

Jesus tells them that He is aware of what they are walking through, including poverty. *Poverty* is the Greek word *ptocheia.* It means "to be beggarly, indigent, and a pauper." Clearly these people as the Church of the Lord Jesus

Christ were in great need. Yet in the midst of this need, Jesus says, "But you are rich!" Wow! So Jesus classified being *rich* not by what they had in their hand but what was in their heart. We are told to be *rich* in many different things. First Corinthians 1:4-7 shows Paul speaking of how *rich* the Corinthians were in the gifting of God.

> *I thank my God always concerning you for the grace of God which was given to you by Christ Jesus, that you were enriched in everything by Him in all utterance and all knowledge, even as the testimony of Christ was confirmed in you, so that you come short in no gift, eagerly waiting for the revelation of our Lord Jesus Christ.*

Their utterance and knowledge that was being released through the gifting of God, Paul classified as riches. The gifts we have from God make us rich. Proverbs 17:8 declares that a gift causes prosperity.

> *A present is a precious stone in the eyes of its possessor;*
> *Wherever he turns, he prospers.*

Prospering is not just about money. It can be about influence gained or impact had. When we value the gifts God has placed in us, we will be enriched and have impact through our utterance and knowledge. The key is not neglecting the gift of God. This is what Paul warned Timothy about in First Timothy 4:14.

> *Do not neglect the gift that is in you, which was given*
> *to you by prophecy with the laying on of the hands of*
> *the eldership.*

To *neglect* means "to have no regard for and to be careless of." We must value and treasure the gifts God grants us. They will make us rich in our impact and influence in culture. They grant us influence money could never give us. The devil knows this; therefore, he seeks to diminish in our eyes the gifts we actually carry from God. Proverbs 20:14 gives us a scenario of someone diminishing what we have so we will *sell* it cheaply or even give it away.

> *"It is good for nothing," cries the buyer;*
> *But when he has gone his way, then he boasts.*

This is what the devil does. He whispers in our ear that what we have isn't valuable and is even good for nothing. We become convinced it is not to be treasured. We therefore begin to neglect what is in us. This is Satan's strategy to make us give away the precious gift granted us from God. We must recognize its immense value. When we treasure it, we become enriched by it. So do the others who are affected by the gift God placed in us. May we with great diligence steward the richness of His gifts in us.

We are told that we are to allow the word of God to be in us with richness in Colossians 3:16. I take this to mean we are to put the word of God into our minds and spirits.

> Let the word of Christ dwell in you richly in all wisdom, teaching and admonishing one another in psalms and hymns and spiritual songs, singing with grace in your hearts to the Lord.

The result of the word of God being richly in us is the ability and power to teach and admonish ourselves and others. When the Word of God is richly in us, the Holy Spirit will bring it forth with great strength to encourage and empower us. It can produce a worship coming from us that greatly impacts us and others. In fact, scripture connects the word dwelling richly in us to the *composing* of psalms, hymns, and spiritual songs. This can speak of prophetic releases that are designed by God to encourage, empower, and shift things in the heavenly realm so things can come to order in the natural. I also believe this is a key to the creating of worship songs that become prophetic anthems in the body of Christ. If someone wants to write worship songs that speak to the body of Christ, they should begin by putting the word of God richly in them. This doesn't mean that songs are simply the repeating of scripture set to music. However, it does mean that the principles of the word of God are contained and echoed underneath the Holy Spirit's unction in these composed songs. They will then move the body of Christ, not just by the music but by the inspired lyrics of the songs. These will come from a heart and soul saturated with the richness of God's word. The result will be a cry released from the heart that will be multiplied many times over throughout the many-membered body of Christ.

Hebrews 11:24-26 tells us that the *reproaches of Christ* are riches to be treasured. This sounds crazy, yet they have great reward when embraced in and through the grace of God.

> *By faith Moses, when he became of age, refused to be called the son of Pharaoh's daughter, choosing rather to suffer affliction with the people of God than to enjoy the passing pleasures of sin, esteeming the reproach of Christ greater riches than the treasures in Egypt; for he looked to the reward.*

When Moses came to maturity, the revelation of who Christ was and therefore who Moses was compelled him to leave the wealth of Egypt and choose rather to suffer with the people of God. The scripture is clear. He did this because he valued the reward attached to the reproach of Christ. Many times people are reproached or taunted and defamed for the cause of Christ. Moses understood there was a tremendous reward for those who chose this instead of the riches of Egypt. Wow! So we also need this revelation. Those who might come to the place of having to make a choice between earthly wealth and the wealth of Heaven must choose Christ. May the same grace that was on Moses be on us to help us choose rightly.

This doesn't mean wealth is wrong. It does, however, mean that should we be placed in a position to choose between earthly possessions and the riches of Heaven connected to being reproached with Christ, we must choose the latter. This is what Moses did. This was also what Jesus required of the one we call the rich young ruler in Mark 10:21-22. When he asked Jesus what he needed to do, Jesus told him to keep the commandments. When he said he had done this since his youth, Jesus then told him to sell everything and give it to the poor.

> *Then Jesus, looking at him, loved him, and said to him, "One thing you lack: Go your way, sell whatever you have and give to the poor, and you will have treasure in heaven; and come, take up the cross, and follow Me."*
>
> *But he was sad at this word, and went away sorrowful, for he had great possessions.*

Out of the love of Jesus for this one, He required him to sell all his possessions and give it away. Jesus realized that the possessions *owned* this person. We are to *own* possessions, not them *own* us. A doctrine cannot be created from this occurrence that demands someone who is rich to give it all away. The reason Jesus required this was because the riches controlled and dominated this man. In other words, they were his lord, rather than God. God must deal with the heart of a person before they can be trusted with riches. If there is any covetousness or greed within the heart, then this must be dealt with. Jesus' promise to this man was if he would obey, then he would have treasures in Heaven. He was not willing to do this and went away grieved and sad. May we care more for riches in Heaven than we do in the earth. Only then can God trust us with wealth and prosperity here. It's always an issue of the heart.

We also find James 2:1-5 shows the scripture seeking to adjust the church's attitude toward wealth, the wealthy, and those who are poor.

> *My brethren, do not hold the faith of our Lord Jesus Christ, the Lord of glory, with partiality. For if there should come into your assembly a man with gold rings, in fine apparel, and there should also come in a poor man in filthy clothes, and you pay attention to*

> *the one wearing the fine clothes and say to him, "You*
> *sit here in a good place," and say to the poor man,*
> *"You stand there," or, "Sit here at my footstool,"*
> *have you not shown partiality among yourselves, and*
> *become judges with evil thoughts?*
>
> *Listen, my beloved brethren: Has God not chosen the*
> *poor of this world to be rich in faith and heirs of the*
> *kingdom which He promised to those who love Him?*

James is uncovering the motive of hearts in this passage. If the rich are given preferential treatment because they are rich, this is wrong. His valid point is that whether rich or poor they should be treated the same. People with money should not be granted privilege in the church because they have money, *and the church / leaders want some of it.* We must *not be for sale!* If we are, then we are not worthy to be a leader in Jesus' church. There are times when people who have money should rightfully be given honor and even places of influence. Their having money can be because they have leadership gifting that has produced this. However, the elevation of such a person should not be because they have finances. To do this is wrong and manipulative. On the other hand, James tells us that the poor God has chosen. They can be rich in faith and they can be heirs of the kingdom of God because they love the Lord. Notice that God doesn't choose them because they are *poor*. He chooses them because they *love Him*. Being poor doesn't qualify us any more than being rich. It is our love and passion for Him that grasps God's attention. However, if in poorness people are serving the Lord diligently, God will make them heirs to His kingdom. There will come a day when the suffering they endured in this life will be rewarded. However, there must be a sincere heart of serving God.

Not everyone is poor because of mistakes they have made. Some are poor because of where they were born. They might be poor because of circumstances thrust on them. Others are poor because of persecution and choices they have made to serve the Lord. These who in the midst of their poverty make Jesus their treasure will be rewarded mightily. We must not make the mistake and think if someone is poor they must be doing something wrong. The early church had begun to adopt this mentality it would seem. First Timothy 6:4-6 gives us further insight into developing a right perspective.

> *He is proud, knowing nothing, but is obsessed with disputes and arguments over words, from which come envy, strife, reviling, evil suspicions, useless wranglings of men of corrupt minds and destitute of the truth, who suppose that godliness is a means of*

*gain. From such withdraw yourself. Now godliness
with contentment is great gain.*

Paul in speaking to his spiritual son, Timothy, wanted
him to have the right perspective. He literally declared
that there were people in the body of Christ who had cor-
rupt minds. One of the incorrect theories they espoused
was godliness was a means to gain or money-getting. This
could mean their theology said that if you were godly you
would be prosperous. Obviously, this is not true from
what we have seen. To judge someone for being poor is
completely and totally incorrect and a stench in the nos-
trils of God. This scripture can also mean that there were
those who were using the church as a money-making
place. In other words, they were making merchandise of
the people of God. They saw God's people as a means to
make a buck. This should never be. The people of God are
to be treasured and valued. They are not to be exploited
for financial reasons. This doesn't mean they shouldn't
give and tithe. As far as I am concerned, giving and tithing are essential parts to securing the blessing of God over
our lives. Not just monetarily but in other areas as well.
These principles actually secure blessings over us and our
generations to come. I mean God's people shouldn't be
seen as business opportunities. They aren't dollar signs.
They are the inheritance of the Lord. Paul then declares
what real *gain* is. It is godliness with contentment. This

means real advantage is when we love godliness and are content with what we have. We aren't greedy or covetous. We are happy and blessed with what God has provided for us. We are not making the accumulation of things our goal in this life. Our desire is to live godly and serve Him with a free heart.

With all of this said, let me now seek to bring a balance. I believe and understand from scripture it is God's passion to bless us financially. What God desires to do in the earth will require a wealthy people (see Deuteronomy 8:18). Plus, the Lord desires us to live a blessed life in this life as well as a full inheritance in the next one. I know there are people who will read this chapter and their attitude will be, "Well, at least he gets that part of it." The religious spirit in them will *confirm* for them their judgments against the *prosperity gospel*. If this is what you get from these concepts I shared, then I have failed. This is *not* my intention. My hope is to give a view of the *other side of the coin*. In the midst of this, I believe God desires His people's prosperity. I actually believe in the *prosperity gospel* as it has been called. Not the one where people are manipulated to give. I hate that. I am speaking of the one where divine principles are taught that position us to receive the blessings of God over our lives and families. I do not believe that being poor is spiritual any more than I believe being rich is. However, I do believe there are certain principles that can be practiced that will produce wealth in the lives of God's people.

In my opinion, anyone who judges people who believe God wants to prosper us is operating in a spirit of religion. This always has a pride and arrogance attached to it. For whatever reason, they consider it spiritual to be poor and in need and take great pride in it. They consider themselves more noble than those of us who would dare contaminate ourselves with the wealth of this world. After all, they want the *real riches* from God. Please give me a break. These judgments are just as horrid in the eyes of God as the ones who would espouse that riches make you better before the Lord.

As one who has been called and functioned in full-time ministry for most of my adult life, I have known the judgments of these people. My family and I have known the pain of lack but also the joy of the blessing of the Lord. I made up my mind years ago that I was not going to allow the judgments of the religious to determine my lot in life. That right belongs to only God and me. For instance, I had seen many ministers' children grow up doing without because their parents were in full-time ministry. I asked of the Lord that my children would not grow up with this experience and the bitterness toward ministry that is quite often associated with it. I wanted my children to consider that they were rather advantaged because we were in ministry. In other words, that we were blessed enough that they got opportunities that others did not get. Now I don't know about you, but that more reflects the Father heart of God toward us than a God who doesn't take care for his own. As a result of this, five of our six children are in full-time ministry in some capacity. Their experience in growing up in a minister's home did not detour them from saying yes to the call of God. In fact, it allowed them to respond to Him and His call without the fear of signing up for a life of lack and need. The result is that the Kingdom of God is being blessed with those who have a passion to serve Him and a confidence in His goodness toward us.

If I had allowed the religious and judgmental people to have pushed their philosophy on me, I promise you this would not be the case. My children grew up with a *good taste in their mouth* concerning ministry and the purpose of God for their life. Part of this was the fact that they saw and partook of the blessing of God that was on our life because of the principles that we obeyed. They saw us believe God and with sacrifice serve Him. They also saw His faithfulness toward us and the way that we have been blessed. All I can say is, "God is good."

One last statement I will make about God's heart to prosper us is that when we walk through places of need and lack, it should be only for a season. It should never become our perpetual lifestyle. Everyone will probably have times when things are tight and even when there is not enough. This should only be for a period of time. It must never become the experience of our whole life, or even a large segment of it. The apostle Paul declared that he went through these places but came out of them. Philippians 4:10-14 gives us insight to Paul walking through these seasonal changes. He knew how to keep the right perspective as he navigated through these places.

> But I rejoiced in the Lord greatly that now at last your care for me has flourished again; though you surely did care, but you lacked opportunity. Not that I speak in regard to need, for I have learned in whatever state I am, to be content: I know how to be abased, and I know how to abound. Everywhere and in all things I have learned both to be full and to be hungry, both to abound and to suffer need. I can do all things through Christ who strengthens me. Nevertheless you have done well that you shared in my distress.

The Philippian church had sent Paul an offering, which had moved him from being *abased* to *abounding*. To be *abased* in the Greek means "to be depressed, to humiliate, and to bring low." It is the Greek word *tapeinoo*. The word *abound* is the Greek word *perisseuo*. It means "to superabound, to be in excess and abundance." Paul moved from a *season* of lack to a *season* of great excess and enlargement. Our season of lack should never last. It should come to an end. If we perpetually live in that place, there is something that is causing it. Perhaps the devil has discovered a legal right to resist your prosperity that God intends. This is the reason for this book. Paul explained how he made this transition. He said he was *content*. He had learned how to find his absolute contentment and joy in who the Lord is and not in what he had.

Contentment is absolutely essential to this transition. In other words, *why* we want riches and wealth is of infinite importance. Do I want riches and wealth so that I will feel good about myself? Do I want riches and wealth so I will know God loves me and is for me? Do I want riches and wealth so others will see me as successful? None of these are valid reasons. All of these can only really be met in a revelation of who Jesus is in our lives and His love for us. Paul had that revelation. Therefore, God could bless him with prosperity. The devil could not use a wrong motive to legally resist God's desire to bless Paul. In other words, only when we find our fulfillment in Jesus can we then righteously handle the wealth and riches God might entrust us with. Our contentment must first come from the Lord and who He is in our life. Luke 12:15 shows Jesus responding to one who was in a place of conflict because he had lost a portion of inheritance.

And He said to them, "Take heed and beware of covetousness, for one's life does not consist in the abundance of the things he possesses."

Only when our lives and hearts are free from covetousness and we are content with what we have can we then move into the place of abounding. My life is not made up of the things I possess. What a shallow and worthless existence. My life is made up of who Jesus is and loving and being loved by Him. The other things I have are just added benefits. They can be used to empower me and help me be a blessing to my family and others. However, if I need them to be happy, then I have yet to have the necessary work done in my heart. We are all in the process. May we become rich toward God in all things that matter, even the financial world, for His glory and purposes to be done.

Lord, as I stand before Your Courts, I ask for the right perspective on wealth to be in my heart. I surrender every insecurity in me that would desire wealth for the wrong reasons. May I be content with such things as I have. May they be used as a means of gratitude and praise coming from my heart to You. Lord, I thank You for Your manifest goodness in my life. May it be recorded in Heaven that I honor You and recognize Your goodness toward me, In Jesus' Name, amen.

CHAPTER 13

GREAT POSSESSIONS SECURED

As we conclude our thoughts, I would remind us of what God promised Abraham concerning his descendants in Egypt. In Genesis 15:13-14 we see God unveiling to him that his descendants would be in captivity in what was Egypt. This is somewhere around 645 years before they will come out of Egypt and make their journey to the Promised Land of Canaan. God is giving Abraham insight into something that will not happen for many centuries to come.

> *Then He said to Abram: "Know certainly that your descendants will be strangers in a land that is not theirs, and will serve them, and they will afflict them four hundred years. And also the nation whom they serve I will judge; afterward they shall come out with great possessions."*

God promises to *judge* Egypt and bring Israel out with great possessions. Of course, the whole idea of something being *judged* involves courtroom activity. The affliction of Israel for the 400 years they were there allowed God the legal right to *judge* Egypt as the righteous Judge of all the earth (see Genesis 18:25). I think it is really interesting that the result of the judgment rendered by God caused *great possessions* to come into the hands of a bunch of people who have served as slaves for 430 years, which was the actual time Israel was in bondage (see Exodus 12:40). The *great possessions* were a result of a legal rendering on behalf of Israel, Abraham's descendants. What is it that allowed this to happen? What granted God the legal right to give a bunch of slaves great possessions and bring them out and into their own land? A judge must have that which will allow this kind of verdict to occur. There is contained in this some wisdom in how to present our own case for *great possessions* to become ours and wealth to be unlocked from the Courts of Heaven.

First of all, the verdict rendered by God as Judge was a result of the covenant He made with Abraham. When God speaks these words to Abraham, it is because He is making a covenant with him concerning his descendants. As I said, it will be somewhere around 645 years before this *prophetic word and promise* comes to pass. Genesis

15:18 clearly states that God at this time made this covenant with Abraham.

> *On the same day the Lord made a covenant with Abram, saying:*
>
> *"To your descendants I have given this land, from the river of Egypt to the great river, the River Euphrates."*

God promised Abraham as his friend that this would happen. Covenant is very important when presenting a case before the Courts of Heaven and the Judge rendering decisions on our behalf. We must always make our appeal to God on the basis of His covenant with us. Covenant is what caused God to remember a bunch of slaves in Egypt 645 years later. The result was great possessions becoming theirs. Of course, we have a covenant with God through the blood and body of Jesus Christ. When Abraham made this covenant with God, it was through the body of slain animals. Genesis 15:8-10 shows God responding to Abraham when he asked how he could know God would keep His word to him.

> *And he said, "Lord God, how shall I know that I will inherit it?"*
>
> *So He said to him, "Bring Me a three-year-old heifer, a three-year-old female goat, a three-year-old ram, a turtledove, and a young pigeon." Then he brought all*

these to Him and cut them in two, down the middle,
and placed each piece opposite the other; but he did
not cut the birds in two.

God made a covenant with Abraham as He walked between the pieces of these slain animals. This was a picture of the covenant that would be made with us through the body and blood of Jesus Christ. If this covenant with Abraham between pieces of animals would cause God to remember Israel and bring them out with great possessions, then how much more our covenant with God through the body and blood of Jesus, the Christ! When God makes a covenant, it is the end of all strife and doubt. In response to Abraham asking for assurance that what they had spoken of would be done, God gave him this covenant. This was to end all questions and fears. So God's covenant with us through Jesus is to end all questions and fears as well. Hebrews 6:16-18 makes an astounding statement about the promise-keeping nature of God.

For men indeed swear by the greater, and an oath
for confirmation is for them an end of all dispute.
Thus God, determining to show more abundantly to
the heirs of promise the immutability of His coun-
sel, confirmed it by an oath, that by two immutable
things, in which it is impossible for God to lie, we

*might have strong consolation, who have fled for ref-
uge to lay hold of the hope set before us.*

God desires to put an end to all disputes, doubts, questions, and fear. He wants it established that He will keep
His word and bring what He promised to pass. He does
this through the establishment of covenant. God's covenant with Abraham ended any and all questions. Notice
that God wants us to have a strong consolation and to
flee into this hope and lay hold of what is set before us.
This is what we have because of the covenant we have
with God through Jesus Christ. There are many benefits
to this covenant, but one of them is great possessions
and the unlocking of wealth for us and our descendants.
God is faithful. He will keep His word. He is our covenant-keeping God who will not fail us. In just a moment
we will see how to present our case before Him as Judge on
the basis of the covenant we have with Him through our
Lord, Jesus Christ.

Another issue in what God promised Abraham was
the affliction that Israel endured for 400-plus years while
in captivity. They *served* Egypt for this time. The Hebrew
word for *serve* and the word *afflict* in Genesis 15:13 is
the same word. It is *anah.* It means "to look down upon
and to browbeat, to depress." This is what happened to
Israel in Egypt. They became the slaves of Egypt and were

oppressed with cruel bondage and hard servitude. Exodus 6:9 actually says that Israel had no ability to respond to Moses when he brought them a good word from God because of their bondage.

> So Moses spoke thus to the children of Israel; but they
> did not heed Moses, because of anguish of spirit and
> cruel bondage.

They were in anguish of spirit and under cruel bondage in Egypt. Even though there were great periods of time when it seemed God didn't see, He was in fact looking. As Judge, God was waiting until the cruelty they were under would *legally* warrant God judging Egypt. God as Judge can only render decisions against something and for something when things fully allow it. We can actually see this as we examine further what He said to Abraham about the timing of his descendants possessing the land. Genesis 15:15-16 reveals that Israel as a nation will not be allowed to take the land from the existing nations that have it until those nations' sin is accumulated to a certain level.

> Now as for you, you shall go to your fathers in peace;
> you shall be buried at a good old age. But in the fourth
> generation they shall return here, for the iniquity of
> the Amorites is not yet complete.

Abraham would live a great life and die with no regrets. His descendants, however, would have to wait until the iniquity of the Amorites, who presently possessed the land, was full. In other words, their sin would give God the legal right to strip the land away from them and give it to Abraham's descendants as an inheritance. Everything that God does must be about justice. When God promises Abraham that He will judge Egypt, this is true too. The Egyptians through their oppression of Israel for 400-plus years will give God the right to judge them and allow Israel to depart with their great possessions. This is why we can come before the Lord and present our case for the unlocking of wealth. We can cite before Him the hardship we have endured. We can present and point out perhaps the generations of poverty our ancestors have suffered. It is quite appropriate before the Lord to bring this to God's remembrance and by faith recite this before Him. This is one of the ways we can request of the Lord a decision that will unlock wealth for us and our generations.

A final thing I would point out that can be a secret to God bringing us into wealth from His Courts is what our petition looks like concerning this. We have seen that reminding God of His covenant with us and reciting the hardship of our own and our ancestors' struggle with poverty is admissible in the Courts of Heaven. The third and final thing connected to Israel gaining great possessions because of the judgment of God as Judge was the *groan* that was presented before Him. Exodus 2:23-25 shows that which caused God to remember His covenant with their fathers and Israel.

> *Now it happened in the process of time that the king of Egypt died. Then the children of Israel groaned because of the bondage, and they cried out; and their cry came up to God because of the bondage. So God heard their groaning, and God remembered His covenant with Abraham, with Isaac, and with Jacob. And God looked upon the children of Israel, and God acknowledged them.*

Notice that God remembered, looked upon them, and acknowledged them because of their *groaning. Groaning* is the sound of pain, but also a cry of faith. We are told in Romans 8:22-23 that our groaning in the Spirit can agree with the groaning of creation that desires to be free from its fallen state.

> *For we know that the whole creation groans and labors with birth pangs together until now. Not only that, but we also who have the firstfruits of the Spirit, even we ourselves groan within ourselves, eagerly waiting for the adoption, the redemption of our body.*

There is a groaning of intercession that will ultimately produce the resurrection of the dead. This resurrection of the dead at the second coming of Jesus will trigger creation being released from its tormented state. This is produced not by some timetable on some celestial calendar but from the groaning of the Spirit in and through the believers. Groanings in God are very important. Romans 8:26 further states that the Holy Spirit produces in us these groanings that allow the will of God to be accomplished.

> Likewise the Spirit also helps in our weaknesses. For we do not know what we should pray for as we ought, but the Spirit Himself makes intercession for us with groanings which cannot be uttered.

As we *groan* in agreement with the passion of God in intercession, what God legally needs is supplied. He can now render judgments in our favor and bring us out with great possessions. This is exactly what happened to the children of Israel. God's covenant-keeping nature mixed with the suffering of the children of Israel and the cry it produced through the Spirit allowed God to judge what was holding them captive. They were freed from their condition and brought into great prosperity as they left the bondage of Israel. As we saw in a previous chapter, Exodus 12:35-36 shows what happened as the Israelites left Egypt.

> *Now the children of Israel had done according to the*
> *word of Moses, and they had asked from the Egyp-*
> *tians articles of silver, articles of gold, and clothing.*
> *And the Lord had given the people favor in the sight*
> *of the Egyptians, so that they granted them what they*
> *requested. Thus they plundered the Egyptians.*

When the children of Israel asked for articles of silver, gold, and clothing, they weren't just given little trinkets. They left with great possessions even as God had promised Abraham when He made covenant with him. This was because of the groaning that actually became testimony before the Lord. According to Revelation 19:10, testimony comes when things are done from a prophetic unction. This is what these groanings are. They are not just the result of pain, discouragement, and perplexity. They are prophetic in nature, agreeing with the passion of the Lord.

> *And I fell at his feet to worship him. But he said to*
> *me, "See that you do not do that! I am your fellow*
> *servant, and of your brethren who have the testimony*
> *of Jesus. Worship God! For the testimony of Jesus is*
> *the spirit of prophecy."*

The *testimony of Jesus* becomes a *spirit of prophecy.* This means that whatever Jesus is presently testifying before the Courts from His place in Heaven becomes a prophetic unction in our lives. This is the groaning that is coming from us as we give birth to wealth God intended us to produce. These groanings can be testimony in the Courts of Heaven that allow God as Judge to render verdicts on our behalf. This is what happened that allowed God to judge Egypt and bring His people forth with great possessions. May it be so with us as well. God needs us to unlock wealth from before the Courts of Heaven so that His passion might be fulfilled. Even so Lord, let it be.

> Lord, as I come before Your Courts, I would remind You of the covenant I have with You because of the body and blood of Jesus Christ. Just like You made covenant with Abraham when You passed through the pieces of slain animals, so covenant has been made with You through Jesus' sacrifice and offering on our behalf. I ask that even as great possessions were produced because of Your covenant with Abraham, Lord, please bring me out of lack, need, and even poverty and into great wealth and prosperity. What You did in a shadow for them, would You do in substance for me (Colossians 2:17)?
>
> Lord, I would also ask that You might look upon my suffering and affliction brought against me

by the spirit of poverty. Every right this spirit would claim against me, would You judge it as illegal and unrighteous. I ask that the hardship I and my ancestors have suffered because of this spirit would now be annulled and over. Free me and my lineage, I ask, from this cruel spirit, even as You freed the Israelites from Egyptian bondage. I thank You that today I go free and come into the great possessions promised through Your covenant. Let the hardships I have endured now speak for me and cause You to remember me and my family.

Lord, I also ask that You would create in me through Your prophetic unction the groaning that will testify before Your Courts. Allow me to groan in agreement with Your passion for this spirit of bondage to be broken. Lord, allow the supernatural cry of Your Holy Spirit to flow through me so that what is necessary might come before Your Courts. As this cry reaches Your ears, O God, please allow a verdict to be rendered that breaks every bondage and brings me into great wealth and possessions for Your glory, honor, and purpose. In Jesus' Name, amen.

ABOUT ROBERT HENDERSON

Robert Henderson is a global apostolic leader who operates in revelation and impartation. His teaching empowers the body of Christ to see the hidden truths of Scripture clearly and apply them for breakthrough results. Driven by a mandate to disciple nations through writing and speaking, Robert travels extensively around the globe, teaching on the apostolic, the Kingdom of God, the "Seven Mountains," and most notably the Courts of Heaven. He has been married to Mary for 42 years. They have six children and five grandchildren. Together they are enjoying life in beautiful Waco, Texas.

INCREASE THE EFFECTIVENESS OF YOUR PRAYERS.

Learn how to release your destiny from Heaven's Courts!

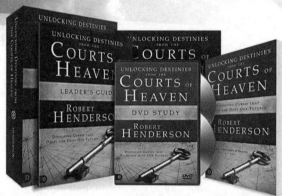

Unlocking Destinies from the Courts of Heaven
Curriculum Box Set Includes:
9 Video Teaching Sessions (2 DVD Disks), Unlocking Destinies *book,*
Interactive Manual, Leader's Guide

There are books in Heaven that record your destiny and purpose. Their pages describe the very reason you were placed on the Earth.

And yet, there is a war against your destiny being fulfilled. Your archenemy, the devil, knows that as you occupy your divine assignment, by default, the powers of darkness are demolished. Heaven comes to Earth as God's people fulfill their Kingdom callings!

In the *Unlocking Destinies from the Courts of Heaven* book and curriculum, Robert Henderson takes you step by step through a prophetic prayer strategy. By watching the powerful video sessions and going through the Courts of Heaven process using the interactive manual, you will learn how to dissolve the delays and hindrances to your destiny being fulfilled.